POPULAR
MUSIC

The Popular Music Series

Popular Music, 1920–1979 is a revised cumulation of and supersedes Volumes 1 through 8 of the *Popular Music* series, of which Volumes 6 through 8 are still available:

Volume 1, 2nd ed., 1950–59   Volume 5, 1920–29
Volume 2, 1940–49   Volume 6, 1965–69
Volume 3, 1960–64   Volume 7, 1970–74
Volume 4, 1930–39   Volume 8, 1975–79

Popular Music, 1900–1919 is a companion volume to the revised cumulation.

This series continues with:

Volume 9, 1980–84   Volume 14, 1989
Volume 10, 1985   Volume 15, 1990
Volume 11, 1986   Volume 16, 1991
Volume 12, 1987   Volume 17, 1992
Volume 13, 1988

Other Books by Bruce Pollock

In Their Own Words: Popular Songwriting, 1955–1974

The Face of Rock and Roll: Images of a Generation

When Rock Was Young: The Heyday of Top 40

When the Music Mattered: Rock in the 1960s

ISSN 0886-442X

VOLUME 17
1992

POPULAR
MUSIC

An Annotated Guide to American Popular Songs,
Including Introductory Essay, Lyricists and Composers Index,
Important Performance Index, Awards Index,
and List of Publishers

BRUCE POLLOCK
Editor

  Gale Research Inc. • DETROIT • WASHINGTON, D.C. • LONDON

Bruce Pollock, *Editor*

Gale Research Inc. Staff

Lawrence W. Baker, *Senior Editor, Popular Music Series*
Allison K. McNeill, *Contributing Editor*

Mary Beth Trimper, *Production Director*
Deborah L. Milliken, *External Production Assistant*

Cynthia Baldwin, *Art Director*
Barbara J. Yarrow, *Graphic Design Supervisor*

Dennis LaBeau, *Editorial Data Systems Director*
Theresa Rocklin, *Program Design*
Benita L. Spight, *Data Entry Supervisor*
Gwendolyn S. Tucker, *Data Entry Leader*
Edgar C. Jackson, *Data Entry Associate*

This book is printed on acid-free paper that meets the minimum requirements of American National Standard for Information Sciences—Permanence Paper for Printed Library Materials, ANSI Z39.48-1984.

Library of Congress Catalog Card Number 85-653754
ISBN 0-8103-8234-2
ISSN 0886-442X

Contents

About the Book and How to Use It

This volume is the seventeenth of a series whose aim is to set down in permanent and practical form a selective, annotated list of the significant popular songs of our times. Other indexes of popular music have either dealt with special areas, such as jazz or theater and film music, or been concerned chiefly with songs that achieved a degree of popularity as measured by the music-business trade indicators, which vary widely in reliability.

Annual Publication Schedule

The first nine volumes in the *Popular Music* series covered sixty-five years of song history in increments of five or ten years. Volume 10 initiated a new annual publication schedule, making background information available as soon as possible after a song achieves prominence. Yearly publication also allows deeper coverage—over five hundred songs—with additional details about writers' inspiration, uses of songs, album appearances, and more.

Indexes Provide Additional Access

Three indexes make the valuable information in the song listings even more accessible to users. The Lyricists & Composers Index shows all the songs represented in *Popular Music, 1992,* that are credited to a given individual. The Important Performances Index (introduced in the revised cumulation, *Popular Music, 1920–1979*) tells at a glance what albums, musicals, films, television shows, or other media featured songs are represented in the volume. The "Performer" category—first added to the index as "Vocalist" in the 1986 volume—allows the user to see with what songs an artist has been associated this year. The index is arranged by broad media category, then alphabetically by the show or album title, with the songs listed under each title. Finally, the Awards Index (also introduced in the cumulation) provides a list of the songs nominated for awards by the American Academy of

About the Book and How to Use It

Motion Picture Arts and Sciences (Academy Award) and the American Academy of Recording Arts and Sciences (Grammy Award). Winning songs are indicated by asterisks.

List of Publishers

The List of Publishers is an alphabetically arranged directory providing addresses—when available—for the publishers of the songs represented in this seventeenth volume of *Popular Music*. Also noted is the organization handling performance rights for the publisher—in the United States, the American Society of Composers, Authors, and Publishers (ASCAP) or Broadcast Music, Inc. (BMI), and in Canada, the Society of Composers, Authors, and Music Publishers of Canada (SOCAN).

Tracking Down Information on Songs

Unfortunately, the basic records kept by the active participants in the music business are often casual, inaccurate, and transitory. There is no single source of comprehensive information about popular songs, and those sources that do exist do not publish complete material about even the musical works with which they are directly concerned. Three of the primary proprietors of basic information about our popular music are the major performing rights societies—ASCAP, BMI, and SOCAN. Although each of these organizations has considerable information about the songs of its own writer and publisher members and has also issued indexes of its own songs, their files and published indexes are designed primarily for clearance identification by the commercial users of music. Their publications of annual or periodic lists of their "hits" necessarily include only a small fraction of their songs, and the facts given about these are also limited. ASCAP, BMI, and SOCAN are, however, invaluable and indispensable sources of data about popular music. It is just that their data and special knowledge are not readily accessible to the researcher.

Another basic source of information about musical compositions and their creators and publishers is the Copyright Office of the Library of Congress. There a computerized file lists each published, unpublished, republished, and renewed copyright of songs registered with the Office since 1979. This is helpful for determining the precise date of the declaration of the original ownership of musical works, but contains no other information. To complicate matters further, some authors, composers, and publishers have been known to employ rather makeshift methods of protecting their works legally, and there are songs listed in *Popular Music* that may not be found in the Library of Congress files.

Selection Criteria

In preparing this series, the editor was faced with a number of separate problems. The first and most important of these was that of selection. The stated aim of the project—to offer the user as comprehensive and accurate a listing of significant popular songs as possible—has been the guiding criterion. The purpose has never been to offer a judgment on the quality of any songs or to indulge a prejudice for or against any type of popular music. Rather, it is the purpose of *Popular Music* to document those musical works that (1) achieved a substantial degree of popular acceptance, (2) were exposed to the public in especially notable circumstances, or (3) were accepted and given important performances by influential musical and dramatic artists.

Another problem was whether or not to classify the songs as to type. Most works of music are subject to any number of interpretations and, although it is possible to describe a particular performance, it is more difficult to give a musical composition a label applicable not only to its origin but to its subsequent musical history. In fact, the most significant versions of some songs are often quite at variance with their origins. Citations for such songs in *Popular Music* indicate the important facts about not only their origins but also their subsequent lives, rather than assigning an arbitrary and possibly misleading label.

Research Sources

The principal sources of information for the titles, authors, composers, publishers, and dates of copyright of the songs in this volume were the Copyright Office of the Library of Congress, ASCAP, BMI, SOCAN, and individual writers and publishers. Data about best-selling recordings were obtained principally from three of the leading music business trade journals—*Billboard, Radio & Records,* and *Cash Box.* For the historical notes; information about foreign, folk, public domain, and classical origins; and identification of theatrical, film, and television introducers of songs, the editor relied upon collections of album notes, theater programs, sheet music, newspaper and magazine articles, and other material, both his own and that in the Lincoln Center Library for the Performing Arts in New York City.

Contents of a Typical Entry

The primary listing for a song includes

- Title and alternate title(s)
- Country of origin (for non-U.S. songs)

About the Book and How to Use It

- Author(s) and composer(s)
- Current publisher, copyright date
- Annotation on the song's origins or performance history

Title: The full title and alternate title or titles are given exactly as they appear on the Library of Congress copyright record or, in some cases, the sheet music. Since even a casual perusal of the book reveals considerable variation in spelling and punctuation, it should be noted that these are the colloquialisms of the music trade. The title of a given song as it appears in this series is, in almost all instances, the one under which it is legally registered.

Foreign Origin: If a song is of foreign origin, the primary listing indicates the country of origin after the title. Additional information may be noted, such as the original title, copyright date, writer, publisher in country of origin, or other facts about the adaptation.

Authorship: In all cases, the primary listing reports the author or authors and the composer or composers. The reader may find variations in the spelling of a songwriter's name. This results from the fact that some writers used different forms of their names at different times or in connection with different songs. These variants appear in the Lyricists & Composers Index as well. In addition to this kind of variation in the spelling of writers' names, the reader will also notice that in some cases, where the writer is also the performer, the name as a writer may differ from the form of the name used as a performer.

Publisher: The current publisher is listed. Since *Popular Music* is designed as a practical reference work rather than an academic study, and since copyrights more than occasionally change hands, the current publisher is given instead of the original holder of the copyright. If a publisher has, for some reason, copyrighted a song more than once, the years of the significant copyright subsequent to the year of the original copyright are also listed after the publisher's name.

Annotation: The primary listing mentions significant details about the song's history—the musical, film, or other production in which the song was introduced or featured and, where important, by whom it was introduced, in the case of theater and film songs; any other performers identified with the song; first or best-selling recordings and album inclusions, indicating the performer and the record company; awards; and other relevant data. The name of a performer may be listed differently in connection with different songs, especially over a period of years. The name listed is the form of the name given in connection with a particular performance or record. It should be noted that the designation "best-selling record" does not necessarily mean that the record was a "hit." It means simply that the record or records noted as "best-selling" were the best-selling record or records of that particular song, in comparison with the sales of other records of the same song. Dates are provided for important recordings and performances.

Popular Music in 1992

Dominated by an Arkansas-born, Elvis-loving, sax-honking, baby boomer's quest for the White House, 1992 saw a rise in the commercial prominence of country music unmatched since the Urban Cowboy rode herd on the record charts in 1980. Similarly aided by Wild Bill's sax solos on television, an entire soundtrack composed of cover tunes in a feature film, and the hotly contested Young vs. Old image battle on a new postage stamp, Presleymania kept pace with this new swing to the country throughout the year. Of even more significance to the genre was the year's dramatic rise in the quality of country songwriting, rivaling the breakthrough efforts achieved by black songwriters in 1990 and 1991.

Ironically, although the most enduring forms of black music—R&B and dance—accounted for more than half of 1992's Top 100 songs for the first time in history, the one song that defined the totality of black songwriting in the national mindset was its most outrageous, rapper Ice-T's blaxploitation epic, "Cop Killer," the ensuing furor over which ultimately caused it to be dropped from its album—much as its writer was dropped from his record label about six months thereafter.

On the troubled rock and roll front, the small city of Seattle had bestowed upon it a disproportionate share of the responsibility for keeping the entire form alive—largely through the efforts of the band Nirvana to identify the aroma of a female deodorant. There and elsewhere, the chalice of defining rock in 1992 was picked up by bands collected under the vague rubric of Alternative; the commercial alternative no longer being MTV, but instead the wide screen at the Cinemaplex, where mass market feature films produced more and bigger hit songs than ever, in effect becoming an alternative to radio's increasingly self-referential and all-too narrow hitmaking machinations.

Popular Music in 1992

Good Ol' Country Comforts

Defying ancient stereotypes, country's leading man, Garth Brooks, leaned perilously toward the progressive camps of folk music, with his paean for racial equality, "We Shall Be Free." Concurrently, heartthrob Billy Ray Cyrus not only achieved a pop penetration unheard of in more than a decade, with "Achy Breaky Heart," but also drove the two-stepping country audience into its own disco craze that resulted in a nightly dance show on the Nashville Channel, delivering a young (or at least youthful) constituency to the music not available since Davy Crockett was defending the Alamo with Walt Disney in the fifties.

At the same time, the voice and considerable persona of one of country's staunchest conservative queens, Tammy Wynette, made "Justified and Ancient," by British band KLF, an alternative masterwork. Returning the favor, the bald-headed beacon of the alternative realm, Sinead O'Connor, covered a Loretta Lynn tune from 1962, Johnny Mullins' "Success Has Made a Failure of Our Home," to somewhat less scintillating effect. On the other hand, the sexually-transcendent k.d. lang achieved a pop breakthrough with her Jo Stafford tones on "Constant Craving," while country anomaly Michelle Shocked, in tunes like "Prodigal Daughter," completed her recent pilgrimage from folk to barndance to minstrel show, in the process revealing as well as reveling in the newfound resiliency of this once-rigid genre.

Further exemplifying how close the country mainstream has drifted toward the muddier waters of folk music, Mary-Chapin Carpenter climaxed a three-year trek into the heartland of mass acceptance, with such superior songs as "I Am a Town," "I Feel Lucky," the acerbic "He Thinks He'll Keep Her," written with Don Schlitz, and "Stones in the Road," legitimized by an interpretation from vintage folk priestess Joan Baez. Carpenter similarly honored Lucinda Williams by covering her "Passionate Kisses," paving the way for Williams' major label debut, with winsome tunes like "Sidewalks of the City" and "Six Blocks Away."

If Bonnie Raitt's successful slide from the gritty neighborhoods of urban folk blues into the countrified pop of "I Can't Make You Love Me," co-written with Allen Shamblin and Mike Reid, can be taken at its most optimistic hearing, then the ear of the marketplace of 1992 has been primed for tunes and messages as difficult and divergent as "Faithless World" by Rory Block, "Bury My Heart at Wounded Knee" by Buffy Sainte Marie, Marty Grebb's "Louisiana Love Call" performed by Maria Muldaur, "Galileo" by the Indigo Girls, "The Dove" by the Roches, and Nanci Griffith's "Gulf Coast Highway," most recently covered by Evangeline, the new band on

Jimmy Buffett's label. Just a bit further down the food chain of accessibility, Suzanne Vega continues to operate at peak proficiency ("Bad Wisdom" and "Blood Makes Noise"), newcomer Tory Amos stuns the heart ("Winter"), Devonsquare warms the fires of nostalgia ("Bye Bye Route 66"), while feisty street poet Brenda Kahn ("I Don't Sleep I Drink Coffee Instead") dubs her urgent stylings "anti-folk."

Along with Garth and Billy Ray, other traditional male voices have come to terms with the changing zeitgeist of Country Music 1992, among them Shenandoah ("Hey Mister I Need This Job") and Travis Tritt ("Lord Have Mercy on the Working Man"). And not far below this popular surface are even more exciting and robust efforts, from singular writers like Lyle Lovett ("Family Reserve"), Larry McMurtry ("Where's Johnny"), Guy Clark ("Picasso's Mandolin"), John Gorka ("The Gypsy Life"), Butch Hancock ("Spit and Slide"), and, most notably, Native American poet John Trudell ("Baby Boom Che"), which evoked the impact of the omnipresent Elvis Presley, both on the culture at large and on the history of the baby boom generation far better than any face on a stamp or tune in a movie, or the applied histrionics of the sax man in the White House.

Let's Hear It for (at) the Movies!

While Presley's songs also dominated the soundtrack of the movie *Honeymoon in Vegas,* including "Are You Lonesome Tonight" by Bryan Ferry, "Can't Help Falling in Love" by Bono Vox of U2, and "Love Me Tender" by Amy Grant (in a separate context, ZZ Top revived "Viva Las Vegas"), country music had an even more prominent showcase in the movie theaters of 1992. Roots-rocker John Cougar Mellencamp did a Paul Simon, writing and starring in a country flavored movie, *Falling from Grace,* which featured a soundtrack of young country stalwarts, most of whom appeared as the Buzzin' Cousins on Mellencamp's "Sweet Suzanne," including Dwight Yoakam, John Prine, Joe Ely, James McMurtry, as well as Mellencamp himself. George Strait starred in *Pure Country,* from which came his hit, "I Cross My Heart," written by Steve Dorff and Eric Kaz. Travis Tritt rewrote "Bible Belt" for the urban vs. rural confrontation comedy, *My Cousin Vinny.* Dolly Parton's *Straight Talk* featured the title tune, among others.

But Parton's biggest success came in a revival of her 1973 tune, "I Will Always Love You," in the movie *The Bodyguard,* not only by ex-X leader John Doe, but also by the film's star, Whitney Houston, whose version went to number one in the country in a matter of a few weeks.

But even this tune was not the top movie song of the year, in a year when such songs had unparalleled access to instant mass acceptance. That honor belonged to the Boyz II Men version of the L.A. Reid/Babyface/Darryl Simmons "End of the Road," from the Eddie Murphy movie, *Boomerang,* a pleasant retro do-wop inspired ballad whose run of thirteen weeks at the top of the charts was longer than any song in Top 40 history (by early 1993, "I Will Always Love You" wound up topping it by a week), besting Elvis's run of eleven weeks with "Don't Be Cruel"/"Hound Dog," and the various runners-up at ten weeks, including perhaps the most justifiably reviled movie song of all-time, "You Light Up My Life," by Debby Boone, as well as "Physical" by Olivia Newton-John, "Singing the Blues" by Guy Mitchell, "Sincerely" by the McGuire Sisters, and "Cherry Pink and Apple Blossom White" by Prez Prado. Three more hits came from the *Boomerang* soundtrack album, Babyface's own "Give U My Heart," "I'd Die Without You," by P.M. Dawn, and Toni Braxton's "Love Shoulda Brought You Home by Now."

Remarkably similar formula tunes were derived from similar formula movies aimed at the black teenage movie-going audience, which is apparently the prime marketplace for sales of Top 40 singles in the 1990s. From *Mo' Money,* Luther Vandross and Janet Jackson sang "The Best Things in Life Are Free" and Color Me Badd, "Forever Love." Jade's "I Wanna Love You" came from *Class Act.* "Mr. Loverman" by reggae legend Shabba Ranks, came from *Deep Cover.* "You Remind Me" by Mary J. Blige came from the soundtrack of *Strictly Business.* Varying a bit from the formula, En Vogue's hit single, "Giving Him Something He Can Feel," written by Curtis Mayfield, was from the 1976 movie, *Sparkle.*

The movie *Juice* gave us a couple of angrier, thus less commercially popular, tunes: Eric B. & Rakim's "Juice (Know the Ledge)," as well as "Uptown Anthem" by Naughty by Nature. Todd Taree, from one of the year's most interesting groups, Arrested Development, wrote "Revolution" for Spike Lee's bio-pic of Malcolm X, in which Aretha Franklin revived the Donny Hathaway/Edward Howard tune, "Someday We'll All Be Free." Aretha also provided one of the finest musical moments of the movie *White Men Can't Jump,* with her rendition of a tune written by its director, Ron Shelton, and music supervisor, Bennie Wallace, "If I Lose Them." Even gospel music got into the act, with Patti Labelle's bravura performance of the Bunny Hull/Ed Reynolds "Ready for a Miracle" from *Leap of Faith,* and the all-white choir, led by Whoopi Goldberg in *Sister Act,* doing the 1963 Peggy March secular hymnal, "I Will Follow Him."

As usual, some of the year's biggest ballads started off as movie songs, including a pair of Disney epics that bookended the year, both composed by Alan Menken: "Beauty and the Beast," which he wrote with his former partner, Howard Ashman, who later died of AIDS, and "A Whole New World," from *Aladdin,* written with *Jesus Christ, Superstar* lyricist Tim Rice. Both tunes were sung by Peabo Bryson (in a duet with Celine Dion on "Beauty and the Beast" and with Regina Belle on "A Whole New World").

In years past, movie music was renown as a customized mixed tape medium of carefully researched (if rarely actually heard) obscure songs that reflected the rarified taste of the director as well as the specific requirements of the film, epitomized by the soundtrack album for Martin Scorsese's *The King of Comedy.* This year, however, movie music became more than ever a haven for pop stars wishing to avoid the rigors of competing with rap, grunge, and dance forms for airplay on the radio. Carly Simon, house songwriter and vocalist for screenwriter/director Nora Ephron, signed on for the title song, "Love of My Life," and several others in *This Is My Life.* Carole King was recruited for "Now and Forever," from *A League of Their Own,* which also contained Madonna's future number one tune, "This Used to Be My Playground." Eric Clapton's wrenching Grammy-winner, "Tears in Heaven," which he wrote with Will Jennings, about the death of his young son, debuted in the mordant film, *Rush.* Later in the year, Clapton teamed up with Sting and Michael Kamen for the jauntier "It's Probably Me," from the appropriately jauntier movie, *Lethal Weapon, Part III.* Freddie Mercury's death from AIDS was eulogized in a couple of movie songs, "The Great Pretender," from *Night and the City,* and "Bohemian Rhapsody" by Queen, the band for which he was lead singer, prominently featured in *Wayne's World.* The movie *Singles* proved its best asset as a showcase for Seattle—the town and its rock scene—underscored by the haunting "Dyslexic Heart" by Paul Westerberg.

More Labels—Alternative and Classic Alternative

As shown in the movie, and heard all over the radio in 1992, Seattle's most significant musical export was not necessarily Nirvana, which followed up "Smells Like Teen Spirit" with a number of similar-sounding drones. Far more creative was Pearl Jam, piloted by Eddie Vedder and Stone Gossard, whose dramatic and powerful songs like "Alive," "Even Flow," and "Jeremy" more fully captured the turbulent feelings of that eternal condition and town.

Fueled by the influx of such true teen spirit, rock bands whose songs could be classified as Alternative fared somewhat better in the marketplace this year than rock bands whose songs were regarded as Corporate (although, by virtue of their very presence in that marketplace of MTV, the charts, and the radio, these tunes were undoubtedly the beneficiary of some corporation or other, priming the marketing pump, regardless of the label put on the product by critics, fans, and other such amateur pop demographers).

In this context, Toad the Wet Sprocket ("All I Want"), the Red Hot Chili Peppers ("Give It Away," "Under the Bridge"), the Spin Doctors ("Little Miss Can't Be Wrong") and the Smithereens ("Too Much Passion") were more than happy to briefly rub shoulders with Paula Abdul, Madonna, and Marky Mark & the Funky Bunch, even if it caused their devoted fans no end of ambivalent judgments on the difference between selling-out and buying-in.

In the realm of Alternative bands whose main difference from the rest of the rock and roll rabble is their ability to appeal to the heightened collegiate rather than the mundane high school sensibility, significant contributions were made by 10,000 Maniacs ("These Are Days"), Soul Asylum ("Somebody to Shove"), They Might Be Giants ("My Evil Twin"), and especially Cracker ("Teen Angst"), with Camper Van Beethoven's main writer, David Lowery, honing his "cowboy on acid" persona into something slightly more salable. Taking the place of the now defunct Camper Van Beethoven as the obscurantist collegiate band of the year was the Lemonheads, whose anthem was "It's a Shame About Ray." For added college credibility (and extra credit), by the end of the year, the Lemonheads would record the Simon & Garfunkel classic "Mrs. Robinson," for inclusion in the new 25th anniversary video edition of *The Graduate*. For a college band, you can't get any more credible than that.

Unless you're from England. In that regard, critics this year bowed down the most to the spare and unrelenting singer, writer and band, P. J. Harvey ("Dress"). All the rave in England was still the techno/disco/acid test flashback Rave scene, in which extended instrumentals and clever sampling techniques ruled the dance floor. It was here where Moodswing got ahold of Jon Anderson and Vangelis ("Spiritual High") and the Utah Saints had their way with Kate Bush ("Something Good"). Elsewhere in the Empire, cult success came to Canada's Barenaked Ladies ("Be My Yoko Ono") and the Irish bar band Black 47 ("Funky Ceili," "Our Lady of the Bronx"), who found success on the streets of New York City.

By far the most compelling story to rise out of this genre, however, is the remarkable amount of legendary veteran acts returning to the scene this year, artists who have devoted their careers to merging the somewhat fey college sensibility with the immediacy and gut-level relevance that has traditionally been thought the sole province of rock, in the process hopefully starting to obliterate and making meaningless the distinction between the two forms. Given the fine format line that still unfortunately existed in 1992 on the radio, as it turns out, more enduring as a symbol of totalitarian mind control than the Berlin Wall and the Iron Curtain, radio stations thus had to compete this year for the right to claim for their airwaves such imposing presences as Tom

Verlaine with the resurrected Television ("Call Mr. Lee"), punk poet Henry Rollins ("Low Self Opinion"), David Byrne, retired again from Talking Heads ("Sax and Violins"), the latest from REM ("Drive"), the return of Bob Mould, with Sugar ("A Good Idea"), and new material from enduring legends of the classic alternative mindset like Lou Reed ("Magic and Loss"), Leonard Cohen ("Democracy"), the late Bob Marley ("Iron Lion Zion"), Peter Gabriel ("Digging the Dirt"), XTC ("The Ballad of Peter Pumpkinhead"), Peter Murphy ("The Sweetest Drop"), Morrissey ("We Hate It When Our Friends Become Successful"), the Cure ("High"), the redoubtable Beastie Boys ("Pass the Mic"), the exemplary Sonic Youth ("100%") and the nearly mythic Tom Waits ("Whistle Down the Wind").

Rock—Music for the Working Class

For a genre perennially thought to be on its deathbed, rock—of the "classic" nature—the primarily teenage beast that runs on hormones and attitude (primarily sexist), meant for the escapist fantasies of a lowbrow and/or working class audience that presumably won't accept anything else, had a banner year in 1992, the banner most often supplied by a corporate mentor whose sole criterion for determining artistic relevance is the amount of beer a band's audience consumes.

In this regard, the anthem of the year had to be "The Majesty of Rock," by Spinal Tap, a fictional band which, in the attempt to reverse the usual process of becoming a recording act after being invented on the screen, immediately went from self-satire to self-parody, while bands like those they used to mock, such as Def Leppard ("Let's Get Rocked"), Damn Yankees ("Where You Goin' Now"), Vince Neil out of Mötley Crüe ("You're Invited But Your Friend Can't Come"), and Van Halen ("Right Now"), plying their trade with no such debilitating ambivalence, fared so much better, financially as well as artistically.

Slightly more devious of intent, many bands this year perfected a formula for luring an unsuspecting young female constituency up to their rooms to hear their love ballads, only to assault their fragile eardrums with an album's worth of their more typical loud white lust. Guns N' Roses ("November Rain"), Mr. Big ("To Be with You"), Saigon Kick ("Love Is on the Way"), the once-dreaded Metallica ("Nothing Else Matters") and even dirty old Ozzy Osbourne ("Mama I'm Coming Home"), benefitted most from this kind of sexist bait and switch. Other rock bands, of a more staunchly unsocialized ilk, refused to compromise the essential male camaraderie of the genre by learning this timeless mating dance. Instead, worshipping speed, anger, and an unyielding social agenda, their songs stayed relatively pure: "Symphony of Destruction" by Megadeth, "Rest in Peace" by Extreme, "Midlife Crisis" by Faith No More, "Would" by Alice in Chains, "Bad Luck" by Social Distortion, "Everything About You" by Ugly Kid Joe, and "Mouth for War" by Pantera.

As a deathbed form, however, it's ironic how much crueler rock is to its elders than any other musical genre, preferring to think of itself as a kind of athletic field of vanishing masculinity where fast-gun rookies are always out to unseat whatever veteran this year shows the least signs of flabby play. Rolling Stone-alone Keith Richards managed to escape this, however, coming through remarkably unscathed for a man his age ("Wicked As It Seems"), while his partner in crime, Ronnie Wood, gained acceptance with the young fraternity of Stones acolytes, mainly through Guns N' Roses dropout Izzy Stradlin's use of Wood's tune, "Take a Look at the Guy," as well as Woody himself on the record. Of course, the Black Crowes continued to parlay their own homage into a prosperous career ("Thorn in My Pride," "Remedy").

From beyond the deathbed, rock relents a bit, awarding immediate and enduring cult status to the dearly departed: Queen ("The Show Must Go On"), Stevie Ray Vaughan ("The Sky Is Crying"), and Bad Company ("How About That")—the last band technically still alive, but creatively dead for many years.

Several other veteran acts put their manhood on the line, vying for a place on this year's all-pro team, with mixed results. While Bruce Springsteen was dismissed as a mere mortal married man ("Human Touch," "57 Channels & Nothin' On"), Neil Young ("War of Man") and Eric Clapton ("Tears in Heaven," "Layla") were roundly accepted for stuff that was easily as mushy. Where U2 ("One") has virtually shed the shackles of its previous "alternative" label, rock's near-willingness this year to open itself up to experimentation allowed such dangerous exemplars of the hated alternative genre as Ministry ("Jesus Built My Hotrod") and Helmet ("Unsung") to drink at the same water cooler. Even rapper Ice-T formed a rock band, Body Count ("There Goes the Neighborhood"). But you have to draw the line somewhere. Although Melissa Etheridge did win a hard rock Grammy for "Ain't It Heavy," it's unlikely any males would actually admit to being in her audience.

R&B—No Dinosaurs Here

Fighting off distractions that would have killed a lesser beast, or any other dinosaur that had become too threatening to the masses, black music continued its impressive evolution in the 1990s. However, its chief cultural engine of rap suffered from massive dilution by savvy marketeers bent on turning it into a Saturday morning cartoon. Of course, in the hands of rogues like Sir Mix-a-Lot ("Baby Got Back"), Wreckx n Effect ("Rump Shaker"), Bobby Brown ("Humping Around," "Good Enough"), Prince ("Diamonds and Pearls") and even the previously neutered Michael Jackson ("In the Closet," "Jam"), it was more like an X-rated cartoon on the Playboy Channel.

But if songs like Carl Martin's "If I Ever Fall in Love" by Shai, the second (or maybe twenty-second) coming of Frankie Lymon, Jermaine Dupri's "Jump" by Kris Kross, Billy Calvin's "Wishing on a Star," an 80's Rose Royce ballad covered by the Cover Girls, "Would I Lie to You" by Charles & Eddie, and "Live and Learn" by Joe Public, sought to return to the music a vestige of its lost innocence, many other black artists realized there was no going back from having tasted the bitter fruit of self knowledge.

With the emergence of the multifaceted Arrested Development ("Tennessee," "Mr. Wendal"), and out of the theatrically oriented "play within a play-on-words" ensemble ethos of A Tribe Called Quest ("Scenario"), newer groups like Me Phi Me ("Sad New Day"), the Disposable Heroes of Hiphopracy ("Language of Violence") and the College Boyz ("Victim of the Ghetto")—appearing on the charts soon after the Rodney King verdict was handed down in Los Angeles—were getting much more of a serious listen from segments of the audience that were previously reluctant to grant them a passing nod.

In the meantime, with the militant wing producing street-informed sagas like "Appetite for Destruction" by NWA, "Shut Em Down" by the enduring Public Enemy, topped off by Ice-T's controversial Body Count ("Wicked," the headline grabbing "Cop Killer," and, in the light of the furor of heartland protests evoked by that song, the prescient revival of his collaboration with the notorious poet/activist, Jello Biafra, "Freedom of Speech"), it was no surprise to find someone like Prince re-establishing his social presence on the cutting edge, with "Money Don't Matter Tonight." But, when as essentially fluffy and mainstream an act as En Vogue ("My Lovin You're Never Gonna Get It") also has a hit with the provocative "Free Your Mind," then you know a new era of introspection is upon us.

Theatre Tunes Dimmed, TV Songs Unplugged

While generally stagnant in 1992, the musical theater did at least provide connoisseurs of the great song with as single a series of moments as were found in any other form this year, in the William Finn opus *Falsettos,* the culmination and coming together of a decade's work, epitomized by such poignant and important songs as "Father to Son" sung by Michael Rupert, "I'm Breaking Down" by Barbara Walsh, and "You Gotta Die Sometimes" by Stephen Bogardus.

Elsewhere on a Broadway where remakes, retreads and retrospectives dominated, *5 Guys Named Moe* took over where 1991's *Jelly's Last Jam* left off, giving us the career of Louis Jordan ("Is You Is Or Is You Ain't My Baby") instead of Jelly Roll Morton ("Chicago Stomp"). The biggest disappointment of the year was the failure of the Lynn Ahrens/Steven Flaherty songwriting team to come up with anything near a repeat of their enchanting *Once on This Island*, with *My Favorite Year*, a vehicle in which the best song may well have been Lainie Kazan's version of "Welcome to Brooklyn."

As usual, more notable work was being done off-Broadway, with significant attention gained by the Joel Paley/Melvin Laird musical, *Ruthless*, from which emanated "Born to Entertain" and "A Penthouse Apartment," and the updated feminist revue, *A... My Name Is Still Alice*, featuring songs from Craig Carnelia ("So Much Rain"), Amanda McBroom ("Wheels"), and Douglas Bernstein and Denis Markell ("Painted Ladies").

Obviously, as Stephen Sondheim learned with Madonna, at least in recent memory, there is no better pipeline to the mass marketplace than the screen, even if it's the small screen. Even if it's on a commercial. This year a Revlon commercial catapulted "Move This" by Technotronic into hit status, and a Volkswagen commercial gave Clannad's ten-year-old "Harry's Game" far more cachet than its earlier-in-the-year appearance in the movie *Patriot Games*. The TV show, "The Heights," produced a number one tune, "How Do You Talk to an Angel," but not enough ratings to last the season. MTV provided a unique new venue for performers in its acoustic show "Unplugged," where Mariah Carey ("I'll Be There") and Eric Clapton ("Layla," "Tears in Heaven") took full advantage. Hoping to follow in the footsteps of Billy Vera, whose "At This Moment" rode prime-time exposure on the sitcom "Family Ties" all the way to the top of the charts in 1987, John Stamos found an old Beach Boys tune, written by the late Dennis Wilson, and used it as his wedding song on "Full House." It was a bomb, although the twins, Ashley and Mary Kate, are reportedly faring much better with their own album and video. Boyz II Men, on the other hand, had a major hit with the R&B chestnut "In the Still of the Night," from the soundtrack of the family epic "The Jacksons: An American Dream." Showing much ancillary promise as a soap opera version of MTV, the teen drama "Beverly Hills 90210" released a soundtrack album filled with potential hits, among them Diane Warren's "Saving Forever for You" by Shanice.

Baby Boomin' Pop

The only trend of interest to report this year in the pop sphere is the ongoing wrenching battle for the very soul of its potential audience. By the nature of its baby boom constituency, the battle, it seems, will continue to be played out for the remainder of the decade, with the entrenched Middle of the Road mentality now in place, being pitted against what I introduced in last year's volume as a "Middle of the Dirt Road" sensibility of songs infused with a distinct baby boom voice that makes use of the incredible amalgam of influences and experiences that have formed the unique and erudite musical taste of this generation. Offering a vision at once harder than country, more realistic than pop, yet definitely beyond the adolescent pandering of rock, this format is already proving to be the repository for the best works of many mature and maturing writers and players, who have moved through other genres and are looking for communication with like-minded, musically knowledgeable peers.

Obviously seeking a foothold on both sides of the generational fence, Michael Bolton, currently the re-incarnation of Tom Jones ("To Love Somebody"), went so far as to collaborate on a song with the nominal fig-urehead of Middle of the Dirt Road, Bob Dylan ("Steel Bars"). Although the tune received much attention, the odd-coupling bespoke chilling echoes of Dylan's 1986 dalliance with the similarly reactionary Carole Bayer Sager on "Under Your Spell."

Yet, with the rejuvenated Kenny Loggins ("Conviction of the Heart"), the happily married Springsteen ("My Beautiful Reward"), the liberated Lindsay Buckingham ("Countdown"), the always poignant Jennifer Warnes ("Lights of Louisianne," "Rock You Gently"), the always pained Loudon Wainwright ("People in Love"), the homey backporch New England of Ed's Redeeming Qualities ("Christmas in Vermont"), the more dismal New England of Bill Morrissey ("Inside"), the lost Greenwich Village of Devonsquare ("Raining Down on Bleecker Street"), Meryn Cadell's caustic stand-up schtick ("The Sweater"), and the naked honesty of the Barenaked Ladies ("What a Good Boy"), this year's contributions to the growing Middle of the Dirt Road cata-log are far from insignificant. Potentially a format with exhilarating latitude, it would also include many of the best songs mentioned earlier. Moreover, it could be the only place on the dial to hear segues like "Bird Alone" by Abbey Lincoln into "Watch the Birds" by Lonette McKee; "Fly Like an Eagle" by the Neville Brothers into "Hail Hail Rock and Roll" by Garland Jeffreys; the Miki Howard revival of Sly Stone's "Thank You for Talking to Me Africa" into Ann Peebles' revival of her own "I Can't Stand the Rain"; the John Hammond, Jr. version of Tom Waits' "No One Can Forgive Me But My Baby" into the Charles Brown rendition of Elvis Costello's "I Wonder How She Knows"; the twisted country of "Church" by Lyle Lovett into the existential west of "Church of Logic, Sin and Love" by the Men; "Breaking the Rules" by Robbie Robertson into "What God Wants, Pt. 1" by Roger Waters; and dusty gems from recent reissues by the Troggs ("Crazy Annie") into Lou Reed ("Little Sister") into the Sex Pistols ("I'm Not Your Stepping Stone").

In the adult format still of record, Middle of the Road, also known as Adult Contemporary, the status remains comfortably quo, with the wallpaper of the New Muzak being applied by diligent if less generationally inspired tunesmiths. Lionel Richie came back in 1992 to reclaim his former love song turf ("Do It to Me"), Elton John and Bernie Taupin cemented their most recent comeback ("The One") and Genesis performed their bi-/tri-annual comeback ritual between solo works without missing a beat or a step ("I Can't Dance"). But the most anticipated comeback by this segment of the marketplace was that of songwriting team Burt Bacharach and Hal David, not only with each other, but with their former prime interpreter, Dionne Warwick, the erstwhile hostess of the Psychic Friends infomercial, on "Sunny Weather Lover," recorded in 1992 for an early 1993 release.

Elsewhere, dreamy ballads continued to dominate the aural terrain, with Diane Warren contributing timeless if redundant material to thrushes as various as Kathy Troccoli ("Everything Changes"), Celine Dion ("If You Asked Me To," "Nothing But My Broken Heart"), Shanice ("Saving Forever for You"), Michael Bolton ("Missing You Now," co-written with Walter Afanasieff), and Michael W. Smith ("I Will Be Here for You"). Sophie B. Hawkins created a brief stir with the edgy "Damn, I Wish I Was Your Lover." Annie Lennox emerged a diva with "Walking on Broken Glass" and "Love Song to a Vampire." Wendy Waldman, once a promising singer-songwriter in the Joni Mitchell confessional mode, continued her transformation into a consummate Las Vegas cum Nashville writer/producer, in the formulaic Vanessa Williams multi-Grammy nominee and chart-topper "Save the Best for Last." Even the once scandalous Patty Smyth found succor in this unchanging realm, in her duet with the previously formidable Don Henley, "Sometimes Love Just Ain't Enough," co-written with Glen Burtnick. All of which served to underscore the notion that Madonna's high ticket infatuation with herself, both in "book" (*Sex*) and song ("Erotica") was, even among this segment of consenting adults, hardly enough to justify our continued unconditional love.

Bruce Pollock
Editor

A

Achy Breaky Heart
Words and music by Don Von Tress.
Millhouse, 1990/Songs of Polygram, 1990.
Best-selling record by Billy Ray Cyrus from *Some Gave All* (Mercury, 92). The Country dance phenomenom of the year, symbolizing country music's latest foray into the mainstream. Nominated for Grammy Awards, Country Song of the Year, 1992, Record of the Year, 1992, and Song of the Year, 1992.

Again Tonight
Words and music by John Cougar Mellencamp.
Full Keel, 1991.
Best-selling record by John Mellencamp from *Whenever We Wanted* (Mercury, 91).

Ain't I a Woman
Words and music by Rory Block and Vinnie Martucci.
Brown Foot Publishing, 1992/Happy Valley Music, 1992.
Introduced by Rory Block on *Ain't I a Woman* (Rounder, 92).

Ain't It Heavy
Words and music by Melissa Etheridge.
MLE Music, 1992/Almo Music Corp., 1992.
Introduced by Melissa Etheridge on *Never Enough* (Island, 92).

Ain't Nobody Like You
Words and music by Lemel Humes.
Virgin Songs, 1992/Buffalo Music Factory, 1992.
Best-selling record by Miki Howard from *Femme Fatale* (Giant/Reprise, 92).

Aint 2 Proud 2 Beg
Words and music by Dallas Austin and Lisa Lopes.

1

D.A.R.P. Music, 1992/Pebbitone Music, 1992/Diva 1 Music,
1992/Tizbiz Music, 1992.
Best-selling record by TLC from *Ooooohhhh....on the TLC Tip*
(LaFace, 92). Nominated for a Grammy Award, Rhythm 'n' Blues
Song of the Year, 1992.

Alive
Music by Stone Gossard, words by Eddie Vedder.
Innocent Bystander Music, 1991/Write Treatage Music, 1991.
Introduced by Pearl Jam on *Ten* (Epic, 91).

All Alone on Christmas
Words and music by Steven Van Zant.
Blue Midnight Music, 1992/Almo Music Corp., 1992/TCF Music
Publishing, 1992.
Introduced by Darlene Love in the film and soundtrack LP *Home
Alone 2* (Fox, 92).

All I Want
Words and music by Dean Dinning, Randy Guss, Todd Nichols, and
Glen Phillips.
Wet Sprocket Songs, 1992.
Introduced by Toad the Wet Sprocket on *Fear* (Columbia, 92).

All Woman (English)
Words and music by Lisa Stansfield, Ian Devaney, and Andy Morris.
Big Life Music, 1991/Careers-BMG, 1991.
Best-selling record by Lisa Stansfield from *Real Love* (Arista, 91).

Alone with You
Words and music by Al B. Sure and Kyle West.
Al B. Sure, 1992/Willarie, 1992/EMI-April Music Inc., 1992.
Best-selling record by Tevin Campbell from *T.E.V.I.N.* (Qwest, 92).

Amigos Para Siempre (Friends for Life) (English)
Words and music by Andrew Lloyd Webber and Don Black.
Really Useful Group, 1992.
Introduced by Jose Carreras and Sarah Brightman as the theme for
The Summer Olympic Games (Really Useful/Polydor, 92).

Anasthasia (English)
Words and music by Olivier Abbeloos and Patrick De Meyer.
D & M Publishing, 1991.
Best-selling record by T-99 from *Children of Chaos* (Columbia, 92).

Annie, I'm Not Your Daddy
Words and music by August Darnell.

Cri Cri Music, 1982/Rainyville Music, 1982/Island Music, 1982.
Revived by Kid Creole and The Coconuts on *Redux* (WB, 92).
Introduced on the album *Wiseguy* (82).

The Answer
Words and music by Garland Jeffreys.
Black and White Alike Inc., 1991.
Introduced by Garland Jeffreys on *Don't Call Me Buckwheat* (RCA, 92).

Anything Can Happen
Words and music by Leon Russell and Bruce Hornsby.
Young Carny Music, 1991/WB Music Corp., 1991/Basically Zappo Music, 1991.
Introduced by Leon Russell on *Anything Can Happen* (Virgin, 92).

Appetite for Destruction
Words and music by Dr. Dre (pseudonym for Andre Young), M.C. Ren, The D.O.C., and Kokane.
Ruthless Attack Muzick, 1991/Dollarz N Sense Musick, 1991/Sony Songs, 1991.
Introduced by NWA on *Efil4zaggin* (Ruthless/Priority, 92).

Are You Happy Now
Words and music by Richard Shindell.
Richard Shindell Music, 1991.
Introduced by Richard Shindell in *When October Goes* (Pluto, 91).
Also on *Sparrow's Flight* (Philo, 92).

Are You Lonesome Tonight
Words and music by Ray Turk and Lou Handman.
Bourne Co., 1926/TRO-Cromwell Music Inc., 1926.
Revived by Bryan Ferry in the film and soundtrack LP *Honeymoon in Vegas* (Epic Soundtrax, 92).

Ashes to Ashes
Words and music by Jakob Dylan.
Brother Jumbo Music, 1992.
Introduced by The Wallflowers on *Wallflowers* (Virgin, 92). Author is Bob Dylan's son.

B

Baby-Baby-Baby
Words and music by L. A. Reid (pseudonym for Antonio Reid),
Babyface (pseudonym for Kenny Edmunds), and Daryl Simmons.
Kear Music, 1992/Green Skirt Music, 1992.
Best-selling record by TLC from *Ooooohhhh....on the TLC Tip* (Laface, 92).

Baby Boom Che
Words and music by John Trudell and Jesse Ed Davis.
Poet Tree Music, 1985, 1991/Blackhawk Music Co., 1985, 1991.
Introduced by John Trudell in *AKA Graffiti Man* (Rykodisc, 92). Originally recorded by Trudell's band, Graffiti Man, on an independent album. Native American poet was one of the most provocative voices of the year.

Baby Got Back
Words and music by Sir Mix-a-Lot.
Polygram International, 1992/Mix-A-Lot Music, 1992.
Best-selling record by Sir Mix-a-Lot from *Mack Daddy* (Def American, 92).

Baby Hold on to Me
Words and music by Gerald Levert and Edwin Nicholas.
Trycep Publishing Co., 1991/Ramal Music Co., 1991/Willesden Music, Inc., 1991.
Best-selling record by Gerald Levert with Eddie Levert from *Private Line* (Atco East West, 91).

Backroads (Canadian)
Words and music by Charlie Majors.
Corner Club Music-Canada (SOCAN), 1991.
Best-selling record by Ricky Van Shelton from *Backroads* (Columbia, 91).

Bad Luck
Words and music by Mike Ness.
Rebel Waltz Music, 1992/Sony Music Publishing, 1992.
Best-selling record by Social Distortion from *Somewhere between Heaven and Hell* (Epic, 92).

Bad Wisdom
Words and music by Suzanne Vega.
WB Music Corp., 1992/Waifersongs Ltd., 1992.
Introduced by Suzanne Vega on *99.9 F* (A & M, 92).

The Ballad of Peter Pumpkinhead (English)
Words and music by Andy Partridge.
Virgin Songs, 1992.
Best-selling record by XTC from *Nonesuch* (Geffen, 92).

Barbie (Canadian)
Words and music by Meryn Cadell.
Meryn Cadell (SOCAN), 1992.
Introduced by Meryn Cadell on *Angel Food for Thought* (Sire/Reprise, 92).

Be My Yoko Ono (Canadian)
Words and music by Steven Page and Ed Robertson.
Treat Baker Music (SOCAN), Ontario, Canada, 1992.
Introduced by Barenaked Ladies on *Gordon* (Sire, 92).

Beautiful Maria of My Soul
Music by Robert Kraft, words by Arne Glimcher.
Warner-Tamerlane Publishing Corp., 1991/Overboard Music, 1991/Isabug Music, 1991.
Introduced by Los Lobos in the film and soundtrack LP *The Mambo Kings* (Elektra, 92). Nominated for a Grammy Award, Best Song for a Movie or TV, 1992.

Beauty and the Beast
Music by Alan Menken, words by Howard Ashman.
Walt Disney Music Co., 1991/Wonderland Music Co., Inc., 1991.
Best-selling record by Celine Dion and Peabo Bryson from the film and soundtrack *Beauty and the Beast* (Walt Disney, 92). Angela Lansbury's vocal in the film won an Academy Award in 1991. Won a Grammy Award, and Best Song for Movie or TV, 1992. Nominated for Grammy Awards, Record of the Year, 1992, and Song of the Year, 1992.

Beneath the Damage & the Dust
Words and music by Peter Himmelman.

Himmasongs, 1992/MCA Music, 1992.
Introduced by Peter Himmelman in *Flown This Acid World* (Epic, 92).
Author is Bob Dylan's son-in-law.

The Best Things in Life Are Free
Words and music by James Harris, III, Terry Lewis, Ralph Tresvant,
Michael Bivins, and Ronnie Devoe.
Flyte Tyme Tunes, 1992/Biv Ten, 1992/Beledat Music, 1992/Rated
RT Music, 1992/Burbank Plaza, 1992.
Best-selling record by Luther Vandross and Janet Jackson (featuring
Bel Biv Devoe and Ralph Tresvant) from the film and soundtrack
LP *Mo' Money* (Perspective/A&M, 92).

Better Class of Losers
Words and music by Randy Travis and Alan Jackson.
Sometimes You Win, 1991/All Nations Music, 1991/Seventh Son
Music Inc., 1991/Mattie Ruth, 1991.
Best-selling record by Randy Travis from *High Lonesome* (Warner
Bros., 91).

Bible Belt
Words and music by Travis Tritt.
Sony Tree, 1991, 1992/Post Oak, 1991, 1992.
Introduced by Travis Tritt in the film *My Cousin Vinnie* (92). A
re-written version was released as a single (WB, 92).

The Big Ones Get Away (Canadian)
Words and music by Buffy Sainte-Marie.
Chrysalis Music Corp., 1991.
Introduced by Buffy Sainte-Marie from *Coincidences & Likely Stories*
(Ensign/Chrysalis, 92).

Big Sky Country
Words and music by Chris Whitley.
Reata Publishing Inc., 1991/Siete Leguas Music, 1991/WB Music
Corp., 1991.
Introduced by Chris Whitley on *Living with the Law* (Columbia, 92).

Bird Alone
Words and music by Abbey Lincoln.
Moseka Music, 1992.
Introduced by Abbey Lincoln on *You Gotta Pay the Band* (Verve, 92).

A Bit of Earth
Music by Lucy Simon, words by Marsha Norman.
Calogie Music, 1991/ABCDE Music, 1991/WB Music Corp., 1991.
Performed by Mandy Patinkin in the cast album of *The Secret Garden*
(Columbia , 92).

Blood Makes Noise
Words and music by Suzanne Vega.
WB Music Corp., 1992/Waifersongs Ltd., 1992.
Introduced by Suzanne Vega on *99.9 F* (A & M, 92).

The Blue Train
Words and music by Jennifer Kimball and Tom Kimmel.
Colgems-EMI Music Inc., 1992/Sweet Angel Music, 1992/Criterion
    Music Corp., 1992/Morrissette Music, 1992.
Introduced by Maura O'Connell on *Blue Is the Colour of Hope*
    (Warner Bros., 92).

Bohemian Rhapsody (English)
Words and music by Freddie Mercury.
EMI Music Publishing, Ltd., London, England, 1975/B. Feldman &
    Co., Ltd., 1975.
Revived by Queen in the film and on the soundtrack LP *Wayne's
    World* (Reprise, 92). Revival of this classic tune benefitted from large
    interest in Freddie Mercury, Queen's lead singer, after he died this
    year of AIDS.

Boot Scootin' Boogie
Words and music by Ronnie Dunn.
Ronnie Dunn Music, 1991/Alfred Avenue Music, 1991/Sony Tree,
    1991/Deerfield Court Music, 1991.
Best-selling record by Brooks & Dunn from *Brand New Man* (Arista,
    91).

Born Country
Words and music by John Schweers and Byron Hill.
Collins Court Music, Inc., 1991.
Best-selling record by Alabama from *Greatest Hits, Vol. 2* (RCA, 91).

Born to Entertain
Words by Joel Paley, music by Melvin Laird.
Introduced by Laura Bundy in the musical *Ruthless*.

Box Set (Canadian)
Words and music by Steven Page.
Treat Baker Music (SOCAN), Ontario, Canada, 1992.
Introduced by Barenaked Ladies on *Gordon* (Sire, 92).

Breakin' My Heart (Pretty Brown Eyes)
Words and music by Larry Waddell, Stokely Williams, and Jeffrey
    Allen.
Flyte Tyme Tunes, 1992.
Best-selling record by Mint Condition from *Meant to Be Mint*
    (Perspective, 92).

Breakin' the Rules (Canadian)
Words and music by Robbie Robertson.
Medicine Hat Music, 1991.
Introduced by Robbie Robertson on *Storyville* (Geffen, 91).

Brian Wilson (Canadian)
Words and music by Steven Page.
Treat Baker Music (SOCAN), Ontario, Canada, 1992.
Introduced by Barenaked Ladies on *Gordon* (Sire, 92).

Broken Arrow (Canadian)
Words and music by Robbie Robertson.
Medicine Hat Music, 1987/EMI-April Music Inc., 1987.
Best-selling record by Rod Stewart from *Vagabond Heart* (Warner
    Bros., 91).

Bury My Heart at Wounded Knee (Canadian)
Words and music by Buffy Sainte-Marie.
Chrysalis Music Corp., 1992.
Introduced by Buffy Sainte-Marie on *The Big Ones Get Away*
    (Ensign/Chrysalis, 92). A noted outspoken writer for Native
    American rights sums it all up again.

Bye Bye Route 66
Words and music by Tom Dean, Alana MacDonald, and Herb
    Ludwig.
Hit List, 1992/Devon Square Music, 1992/MDL Publishing,
    1992/Venutian Publishing Ltd, 1992.
Introduced by Devonsquare on *If You Could See Me Now* (Atlantic,
    92).

C

Cadillac Style
Words and music by Mark Petersen.
Ray Stevens Music, 1991.
Best-selling record by Sammy Kershaw from *Don't Go Near the Water* (Mercury, 91).

Cafe on the Corner
Words and music by Mac McAnally.
Beginner Music, 1992.
Introduced by Sawyer Brown on *Dirt Road* (Curb, 92).

California Here I Come
Words and music by Sophie B. Hawkins.
Broken Plate Music Inc., 1991/The Night Rainbow Music, 1991.
Introduced by Sophie B. Hawkins in *Tongues and Tails* (Columbia, 92).

Call Mr. Lee
Words and music by Tom Verlaine, words and music by Television.
Ohoo Music, 1992.
Introduced by Television on *Television* (Capitol, 92). Long-awaited comeback from seminal art/punk band from the '70s.

Calling All Angels (Canadian)
Words and music by Jane Siberry.
Wing It, 1991.
Introduced by Jane Siberry with k.d. lang in the film and soundtrack LP *Until the End of the World* (Reprise, 91).

Calling Elvis (English)
Words and music by Mark Knopfler.
Chariscourt Ltd., 1991/Almo Music Corp., 1991.
Introduced by Dire Straits in *On Every Street* (Warner Bros., 92).

Can't Cry Hard Enough
Words and music by David Williams and Marvin Etzioni.
PSO Ltd., 1991/Blue Saint Music, 1991/Sky Garden Music,
    1991/Prophet Sharing Music, 1991.
Introduced by The Williams Brothers in *The Williams Brothers*
    (Warner Bros., 91).

Can't Help Falling in Love
Words and music by George Weiss, Hugo Peretti, and Luigi Creatore.
Gladys Music, 1961.
Revived by Bono for the film and soundtrack LP *Honeymoon in Vegas*
    (Epic Soundtrack, 92).

Can't Let Go
Words and music by Mariah Carey and Walter Afanasieff.
M. Carey Songs, 1991/WB Music Corp., 1991/Wallyworld Music,
    1991/Sony Songs, 1991.
Best-selling record by Mariah Carey from *Emotions* (Columbia, 91).

Caribbean Blue (Irish)
Words by Roma Ryan, music by Enya.
EMI Songs Ltd., 1991.
Introduced by Enya in *Shepherd Moons* (Reprise, 91).

Carry On
Words and music by Eric Beall.
Irving Music Inc., 1992.
Introduced by Martha Wash on *Martha Wash* (RCA, 92).

Check out the Radio
Words and music by Hank Boxley, Keith Boxley, and Aaron Allen.
Falterious, 1984/Songs of Polygram, 1984.
Revived by Spectrum City in the film and soundtrack LP *South
    Central* (Hollywood/Basic, 92).

Chicago Stomp
Words by Susan Birkenhead, words and music by Jellyroll Morton,
    music by Luther Henderson.
Edwin H. Morris, 1991.
Introduced by the cast of the musical *Jelly's Last Jam* (Mercury, 92).

Christmas in Vermont
Words and music by Ed's Redeeming Qualities.
Ed's Quality Music, 1991.
Introduced by Ed's Redeeming Qualities on *It's All Good News* (Flying
    Fish, 91).

Church
Words and music by Lyle Lovett.
Michael H. Goldsen, Inc., 1992/Lyle Lovett, 1992.
Introduced by Lyle Lovett on *Joshua Judges Ruth* (Curb/MCA, 92).

Church of Logic, Sin & Love
Words and music by Jef Scott.
Entertainment Management Services Inc., 1992.
Introduced by The Men on *The Men* (Polydor, 92).

Cigarette Ashes on the Floor
Words and music by Miki Howard and Graig T. Cooper.
Mardago Music, 1992/Peermusic Ltd., 1992/Copick Music,
    1992/PSO Ltd., 1992.
Introduced by Miki Howard on *Femme Fatale* (Giant, 92).

Clean up Man
Words and music by Willie D.
N-The Water Publishing, 1992.
Introduced by Willie D. from *I'm Goin' out Lika Soldier*
    (Rap-A-Lot/Priority, 92).

The Closing of the Year (English)
Words and music by Trevor Horn and Hans Zimmer.
Fox Film Music Corp., 1992/Unforgettable Songs, 1992/Zoe Zimmer
    Music, 1992.
Introduced by Wendy & Lisa & the cast of *Toys* in the film and
    soundtrack LP *Toys* (Geffen, 92).

Come & Talk to Me
Words and music by DeVante Swing.
EMI-April Music Inc., 1991/Deswing Mob, 1991/Across 110th
    Street, 1991.
Best-selling record by Jodeci from *Forever My Lady* (Uptown, 91).

Come as You Are
Words and music by Kurt Cobain, words and music by Nirvana.
Virgin Songs, 1991/End of Music, 1991.
Best-selling record by Nirvana from *Nevermind* (PGC, 91). Most
    popular representative of the "Seattle Sound" continued to ride on
    last year's reputation.

Come in out of the Rain
Words and music by Don Pfrimmer and Frank Myers.
GID Music Inc., 1991/Dixie Stars Music, 1991/Josh-Nick Music,
    1991.
Best-selling record by Doug Stone from *I Thought It Was You* (Epic,
    91).

13

The Comfort Zone
Words and music by Kipper Jones and Reggie Stewart.
Pecot Music, 1991/Kipteez Music, 1991/Virgin Music, Inc.,
    1991/Something Stoopid Music, 1991/Almo Music Corp., 1991.
Best-selling record by Vanessa Williams from *The Comfort Zone*
    (Wing, 91).

Constant Craving (Canadian)
Words and music by k. d. lang and Ben Mink.
Bumstead (SOCAN), British Columbia, Canada, 1992/Zavion
    (SOCAN), British Columbia, Canada, 1992.
Introduced by k.d. lang on *Ingenue* (Sire, 92). Critical country pop
    breakthrough for ru le-breaking gender and genre-bender.
    Nominated for Grammy Awards, Record of the Year, 1992, and
    Song of the Year, 1992.

Conviction of the Heart
Words and music by Kenny Loggins.
Milk Money Music, 1991.
Introduced by Kenny Loggins on *Leap of Faith* (Columbia, 91).

Cop Killer
Words and music by Ice-T.
Rhyme Syndicate, 1992.
Introduced by Body Count on *Body Count* (Sire/Warner Brothers, 92).
    Year's most controversial rap espousing violence, came to
    prominence in the wake of the Rodney King verdict. Due to protest
    by the police, song was eventually pulled from the album.

Could've Been Me
Words and music by Reid Neilson and Monty Powell.
Englishtown, 1992/Warner-Tamerlane Publishing Corp., 1992.
Best-selling record by Billy Ray Cyrus from *Some Gave All* (Mercury,
    92).

Countdown
Words and music by Lindsay Buckingham.
Now Sounds Music, 1992.
Introduced by Lindsay Buckingham on *Out of the Cradle* (Reprise, 92).

Cradle of the Interstate
Words and music by Nancy Griffith.
Ponder Heart Music, 1991/Irving Music Inc., 1991.
Introduced by Nancy Griffith in the film and soundtrack LP *Falling*
    from Grace (Mercury, 92).

Crazy Annie
Words and music by Chip Taylor.

EMI-Blackwood Music Inc., 1970.
Introduced by The Troggs on *Athens Andover* (Rhino, 92). Taylor
  wrote their original anthem, "Wild Thing."

Crucify
Words and music by Tori Amos.
Sword and Stone, 1991.
Introduced by Tori Amos in *Little Earthquakes* (Atlantic, 92). The
  confessional singer-songwriter returns, guiltier than ever.

D

Dallas
Words and music by Alan Jackson and Keith Stegall.
Mattie Ruth, 1991/Seventh Son Music Inc., 1991/Warner-Tamerlane
Publishing Corp., 1991.
Best-selling record by Alan Jackson from *Don't Rock the Jukebox*
(Arista, 91).

Damn, I Wish I Was Your Lover
Words and music by Sophie B. Hawkins.
Broken Plate Music Inc., 1992/The Night Rainbow Music, 1992.
Best-selling record by Sophie B. Hawkins from *Tongues and Tails*
(Columbia, 92).

Dance without Sleeping
Words and music by Melissa Etheridge, Kevin McCormick, and
Maurice Fritz Lewak.
MLE Music, 1992/Almo Music Corp., 1992/Eye Cue Music, 1992.
Introduced by Melissa Etheridge on *Never Enough* (Island, 92).

Deeper and Deeper
Words and music by Madonna Ciccone, Shep Pettibone, and Tony
Shimkin.
WB Music Corp., 1992/Webo Girl, 1992/Shepsongs, 1992/MCA
Music, 1992.
Best-selling record by Madonna from *Erotica* (Maverick/Sire, 92).

Democracy (Canadian)
Words and music by Leonard Cohen.
Leonard Cohen Stranger Music Inc., 1992.
Introduced by Leonard Cohen on *The Future* (Columbia, 92). Weighty
words from pop's poet-philosopher in residence.

Diamonds and Pearls
Words and music by Prince, words and music by New Power
 Generation.
Controversy Music, 1991/WB Music Corp., 1991.
Best-selling record by Prince & the New Power Generation from
 Diamonds and Pearls (Paisley Park, 91).

Dig My Do
Words and music by Maureen McElheron.
No publisher available.
Introduced by Chris Hoffman in the film *The Tune.*

Digging the Dirt (English)
Words and music by Peter Gabriel.
Real World Music, 1992/Hidden Pun, 1992.
Introduced by Peter Gabriel in *Us* (Geffen, 92). Another victim of the
 confessional mode. Nominated for a Grammy Award, Best Rock
 Song of the Year, 1992.

The Dirt Road
Words and music by Mark Miller and Gregg Hubbard.
Zoo II Music, 1992/Myrt & Chuck's Boy Music, 1992.
Best-selling record by Sawyer Brown from *Dirt Road* (Curb, 92).

Divine Things (English)
Words and music by Sean Dickson.
Big Life Music, 1992/Playful Music, 1992/Warner-Tamerlane
 Publishing Corp., 1992.
Best-selling record by the Soup Dragons from *Hot Wired* (Big Life, 92).
 Featured in the film a nd soundtrack LP *Hell Raiser III* (Columbia,
 92).

Dizz Knee Land
Words and music by Joie Alio and Michael Gorley.
I.R.S., 1992/Pop's Morgan Music, 1992/Thumb Sucker Music, 1992.
Introduced by dada on *Puzzle* (I.R.S., 92).

Do I Have to Say the Words (Canadian-English)
Words and music by Bryan Adams, Robert John Lange, and Jim
 Vallance.
Badams, 1992/Almo Music Corp., 1992/Zomba Enterprises, Inc.,
 1992/Testatyme, 1992.
Best-selling record by Bryan Adams from *Wakin' up the Neighborhood*
 (A & M, 92).

Do It to Me
Words and music by Lionel Richie.

Speeding Bullet Music, 1992.
Best-selling record by Lionel Richie from *Back to Front* (Motown, 92).

Do You Believe in Us
Words and music by Jon Secada and Miguel Morejon.
Estefan Music, 1992/Foreign Imported, 1992.
Best-selling record by Jon Secada from *Jon Secada* (SBK, 92).

Don't Be Afraid
Words and music by Hank Schocklee, Gary G. Wiz, Floyd Fisher, and Aaron Hall.
Shocklee, 1991/Nasty Man Music, 1991.
Best-selling record by Aaron Hall in the film and soundtrack LP *Juice* (Soul, 91).

Don't Let Our Love Start Slippin' Away
Words and music by Vince Gill and Pete Wasner.
Benefit, 1992/Foreshadow Songs, Inc., 1992/Uncle Pete Music, 1992.
Best-selling record by Vince Gill from *I Still Believe in You* (MCA, 92).

Don't Think About Her When You're Trying to Drive
Words and music by Ry Cooder, John Hiatt, Jim Keltner, and Nick Lowe.
Plangent Visions Music, Inc., London, England, 1992/Tonopah & Tidewater Music, 1992/Whistling Moon Traveler, 1992/Careers-BMG, 1992/Oooeee Music, 1992.
Introduced by Little Village on *Little Village* (Reprise, 92). Politically correct supergroup of musicians' musicians.

The Dove
Words and music by Maggie Roche.
Deshufflin' Inc., 1992.
Introduced by The Roches on *The Dove* (MCA, 92).

Dress (English)
Words and music by Polly Jean Harvey and Robert Ellis.
Harvey (England), England, 1991.
Introduced by P. J. Harvey on *Dry* (Indigo/Island, 92).

Drive
Words and music by William Berry, Peter Buck, Mike Mills, and Michael Stipe.
Night Garden Music, 1992/In This World Music, 1992/Among Others Music, 1992/Unichappell Music Inc., 1992.
Best-selling record by R.E.M. from *Automatic for the People* (Warner Bros., 92).

Dusty Pages
Words and music by James McMurtry.
Short Trip Music, 1992/Bug Music, 1992.
Introduced by James McMurtry on *Candyland* (Columbia, 92). Author is the son of novelist Larry McMurtry.

Dyslexic Heart
Words and music by Paul Westerberg.
NAH Music, 1992.
Introduced by Paul Westerberg in the film and on the soundtrack LP *Singles* (Epic Sountrax, 92). Signature song from leader of proto post-garage/punk band The Replacements displaces a Minneapolis attitude into a trendy Seattle movie.

E

End of the Road
Words and music by L. A. Reid (pseudonym for Antonio Reid),
　Babyface (pseudonym for Kenny Edmunds), and Daryl Simmons.
Kear Music, 1992/Green Skirt Music, 1992/Ensign Music Corp.,
　1992.
Introduced by Boyz II Men in the film and soundtrack LP *Boomerang*
　(Gee Street/LaFace, 92). Song occupied the number one spot on the
　charts longer than any other in popular history. Nominated for a
　Grammy Award, Best Rhythm 'n' Blues Song of the Year, 1992.

Erotica
Words and music by Madonna Ciccone and Shep Pettibone.
WB Music Corp., 1992/Bleu Disque Music, 1992/Webo Girl,
　1992/Shepsongs, 1992/MCA Music, 1992.
Best-selling record by Madonna from *Erotica* (Maverick/Sire, 92). The
　recorded version of Madonna's obsessive book, Sex.

Even Better Than the Real Thing (Irish)
Words and music by U2.
Chappell & Co., Inc., 1991.
Best-selling record by U2 from *Achtung Baby* (Island, 91).

Even Flow
Words and music by Stone Gossard and Eddie Vedder.
Innocent Bystander Music, 1991/Write Treatage Music, 1991.
Introduced by Pearl Jam on *Ten* (Epic, 91). One of Seattle's staunchest
　bands.

Every Second
Words and music by Wayne Perry and Gerald Smith.
Zomba Enterprises, Inc., 1992/O-Tex, 1992.
Best-selling record by Collin Raye from *All I Can Be* (Epic, 91).

Everything About You
Words and music by Klaus Eichstadt and Whitfield Crane.
Sloppy Slouch Music, 1992.
Best-selling record by Ugly Kid Joe from *As Ugly As They Wanna Be*
(Stardog, 92).

Everything Changes
Words and music by Diane Warren.
Realsongs, 1992.
Best-selling record by Kathy Troccoli from *Pure Attraction*
(Reunion/Geffen, 92).

F

Face to Face (American-English)
Words and music by Danny Elfman, words and music by Siouxsie &
 The Banshees.
Dreamhouse (England), England, 1992/Warner-Tamerlane
 Publishing Corp., 1992/Little Maestro Music, 1992.
Introduced by Siouxsie & The Banshees in the film and soundtrack LP
 Batman Returns (Warner Bros., 92).

Faithful (English)
Words and music by Pete Cox, Richard Drummie, and Martin Page.
Dodgy Music, 1992/EMI-April Music Inc., 1992/Martin Page,
 1992/Famous Music Corp., 1992.
Best-selling record by Go West from *Go West* (EMI/ERG, 92).

Faithless World
Words and music by Rory Block.
Brown Foot Publishing, 1992/Happy Valley Music, 1992.
Introduced by Rory Block on *Ain't I a Woman* (Rounder, 92).

Family Reserve
Words and music by Lyle Lovett.
Michael H. Goldsen, Inc., 1992/Lyle Lovett, 1992.
Introduced by Lyle Lovett on *Joshua Judges Ruth* (Curb/RCA, 92).
 Country's premier twisted wordsmith travels into Faulknerian
 territory.

Father to Son
Words and music by William Finn.
No publisher available.
Introduced by Michael Rupert in *Falsettos* (92).

Feels So High (English)
Words and music by Des'ree Weeks and Michael Graves.

Sony Songs, 1988, 1992/WB Music Corp., 1988, 1992.
Best-selling record by Des'ree from *Mind Adventures* (Epic/Sony, 92).

57 Channels (and Nothin' On)
Words and music by Bruce Springsteen.
Bruce Springsteen Publishing, 1989.
Introduced by Bruce Springsteen on *Human Touch* (Columbia, 92).
The Boss's commentary on the joy and pain of domestic life in the
Age of Technology.

Fight the Youth
Words and music by Kendall Jones, John Norwood Fisher, and
Philip Fisher.
Bouillabaisse Music, 1991/Music Corp. of America, 1991.
Introduced by Fishbone in *The Reality of My Surroundings* (Columbia,
91).

Five Guys Named Moe
Words and music by Larry Wynn and Jerry Bresler.
Leeds Music Corp., 1941/MCA Music, 1941.
Introduced by the cast of *Five Guys Named Moe* (Columbia, 92), a
musical based on the life of influencial bandleader Louis Jordan.

Five Women
Words and music by Prince.
Controversy Music, 1992.
Performed by Joe Cocker on *Night Calls* (Capitol, 92).

Flesh and Blood
Words and music by Wilson Phillips, words and music by Glen
Ballard.
EMI-Blackwood Music Inc., 1992/Aerostation Corp., 1992/Get Out
Songs, 1992/Smooshie Music, 1992/MCA Music, 1992/Lentle
Music, 1992.
Introduced by Wilson Phillips on *Shadows and Light* (SBK, 92).

Flex (Jamaican)
Words and music by Ewart Brown, Clifton Dillon, and B. Thompson.
Aunt Hilda's Music, 1992/Zomba Enterprises, Inc., 1992/Shadows
International, 1992.
Best-selling record by The Mad Cobra in *Hard to Wet, Easy to Dry*
(Columbia, 92).

Fly Like an Eagle
Words and music by Steve Miller.
Sailor Music, 1976.
Revived by The Neville Brothers on *Family Groove* (A & M, 92).

Fone Sex
Words and music by Man Parrish and Cherry Vanilla.
Vanilla Music, 1991/Girlfriend Music, 1991.
Introduced by Cherry Vanilla and Man Parrish on *If You Think You're Nasty* (Radikal, 91). An astute commentary on the joy and pain of safe sex in the '90s.

Fora da Ordem (Portuguese)
Portuguese words and music by Caetano Veluso.
No publisher available.
Introduced by Caetano Veluso on *Circulado* (Elektra/Nonesuch, 92). Author is regarded as the Bob Dylan of Brazil.

Forever
Words and music by Dennis Wilson and Greg Jakobson.
Daywin Music, Inc., 1970, 1992/Careers-BMG, 1970, 1992/Brother Music, 1970, 1992.
Introduced by John Stamos with the Beach Boys on *Full House;* also on Beach Boys *Summer in Paradise* (Brother Entertainment, 92). Written by the late Dennis Wilson in 1970, but not previously released, this tune was used as the wedding song of Jesse and Becky on the sit-com *Full House.*

Forever Love
Words and music by Color Me Badd, words and music by James Harris, III and Terry Lewis.
Me Good, 1992/Flyte Tyme Tunes, 1992/Burbank Plaza, 1992.
Best-selling record by Color Me Badd from the film and soundtrack LP *Mo' Money* (Giant, 92).

Free Your Mind
Words and music by Thom McElroy and Denzil Foster.
Irving Music Inc., 1992.
Best-selling record by En Vogue from *Funky Divas of Soul* (Atco East West, 92).

Freedom of Speech
Words and music by Ice-T.
Colgems-EMI Music Inc., 1989/Rhyme Syndicate, 1989.
Revived by Body Count on *Body Count* (Warner Bros., 92). Vocal by Jello Biafra. Apt re-release by the outspoken rapper Ice-T's rock band, with words by a noted poet and cult figure, Biafra.

Friday I'm in Love (English)
Words and music by Robert Smith, Simon Gallup, Purl Thompson, Boris Williams, and Perry Bamonte.

Fiction Songs U.S. Inc., 1992.
Best-selling record by The Cure from *Wish* (Elektra Fiction, 92).

Friend Like Me
Music by Alan Menken, words by Howard Ashman.
Walt Disney Music Co., 1992/Wonderland Music Co., Inc., 1992.
Introduced in the film and soundtrack of *Aladdin* (Walt Disney, 92).
  Nominated for an Academy Award, Best Song of the Year, 1992.

Funky Ceili (Bridie's Song)
Words and music by Larry Kirwan.
Starry Plough Music, 1992.
Introduced by Black 47 in *Black 47* (SBK/Eng, 92). Transplanted Irish
  pub-rockers.

G

Galileo
Words and music by Emily Saliers.
Virgin Songs, 1992/Godhap Music, 1992.
Best-selling record by Indigo Girls from *Rites of Passage* (Epic, 92).
 The perils of re-incarnation by the female Simon & Garfunkel.

Games
Words and music by Chuckii Booker, Gerald Levert, and C. J.
 Anthony.
Count Chocula Music, 1992/Trycep Publishing Co., 1992/Black Satin
 Music, 1992/Big Giant Music, 1992/Warner-Tamerlane Publishing
 Corp., 1992.
Best-selling record by Chuckii Booker from *Nice N' Wild* (Atlantic,
 92).

Ghost
Words and music by Emily Saliers.
Godhap Music, 1992/Virgin Songs, 1992.
Introduced by Indigo Girls on *Rites of Passage* (Epic, 92).

Girlfriend
Words and music by Matthew Sweet.
EMI-Blackwood Music Inc., 1989/Charm Trap Music, 1989.
Introduced by Matthew Sweet on *Girlfriend* (Zoo, 91).

The Girls in My Life
Words and music by Randy Newman.
Randy Newman Music, 1992.
Introduced by Randy Newman in concert performance. Part of a song
 cycle based on the Faust Legend.

Give U My Heart
Words and music by Bo Watson, Babyface (pseudonym for Kenny Edmunds), Daryl Simmons, and L. A. Reid (pseudonym for Antonio Reid).
Kear Music, 1992/Ensign Music Corp., 1992/Green Skirt Music, 1992/Saba Seven Music, 1992.
Best-selling record by Babyface (featuring Toni Braxton) from the film and soundtrack *Boomerang* (Gee Street/Laface, 92).

Giving Him Something He Can Feel, also known as **Something He Can Feel**
Words and music by Curtis Mayfield.
Warner-Tamerlane Publishing Corp., 1976.
Revived by En Vogue on *Funky Divas of Soul* (Atco, 92). Introduced by Lonette McKee in the 1976 movie *Sparkle*. Best-selling record by Aretha Franklin in 1976.

God Save the Queen (English)
Words and music by Paul Cook, Steve Jones, Glen Matlock, and Johnny Rotten.
Glitterbest Music, 1978/Careers-BMG, 1978/WB Music Corp., 1978.
Revived by The Sex Pistols in the film and soundtrack LP *The Great Rock 'n' Roll Swindle* (WB, 92). Reliving the days of punk rock's most reviled specimens in song and film.

Goin out West
Words and music by Tom Waits.
Jalma, 1992.
Introduced by Tom Waits on *Bone Machine* (Island, 92). Nearly accessible sentiments from the Kerouac of jukebox jive.

Good Enough
Words and music by Babyface (pseudonym for Kenny Edmunds), L. A. Reid (pseudonym for Antonio Reid), and Daryl Simmons.
Kear Music, 1992/Green Skirt Music, 1992.
Best-selling record by Bobby Brown from *Bobby* (MCA, 92).

Good for Me
Words and music by Tom Snow, Jay Gruska, Amy Grant, and Wayne Kirkpatrick.
Age to Age, 1991/J-88 Music, 1991/Tom Snow Music, 1991/Emily Boothe, 1991/Geffen Music, 1991.
Best-selling record by Amy Grant from *Heart in Motion* (A & M, 91).

A Good Idea
Words and music by Bob Mould.

Granary Music, 1992.
Introduced by Sugar on *Copper Blue* (Rykodisc, 92).

Good Old World
Words and music by Tom Waits and Kathleen Brennan.
Jalma, 1991/Ackee Music Inc., 1991.
Introduced by Tom Waits in the film and soundtrack LP *Night on Earth* (Island, 92).

Good Stuff
Words and music by The B-52's.
More Gliss Music, 1991/Irving Music Inc., 1991.
Best-selling record by The B-52's from *Good Stuff* (Reprise, 92).

Goodbye
Words and music by Kyle West and Al B. Sure.
Al B. Sure, 1991/Willarie, 1991.
Best-selling record by Tevin Campbell from *T.E.V.I.N.* (Qwest, 91).

The Great Pretender
Words and music by Buck Ram.
Panther Music Corp., 1955/Southern Music Publishing Co., Inc., 1955.
Revived by Freddie Mercury in the film and on the soundtrack LP *Night & The City* (Hollywood, 92).

The Greatest Man I Never Knew
Words and music by Rich Leigh and Layng Martine, Jr.
EMI-April Music Inc., 1992/Lion Hearted Music, 1992/Layng Martine Jr. Songs, 1992.
Best-selling record by Reba McEntire from *For My Broken Heart* (MCA, 92). Nominated for a Grammy Award, Country Song of the Year, 1992.

Gulf Coast Highway
Words and music by Nancy Griffith, James Hooker, and Danny Flowers.
Wing & Wheel, 1988/Irving Music Inc., 1988/Rick James Music, 1988/Danny Flowers, 1988/Bug Music, 1988.
Performed by Evangeline on *Evangeline* (Margaritaville, 92).

Gun Love
Words and music by Billy Gibbons, Dusty Hill, and Frank Beard.
Hamstein Music, 1992.
Best-selling record by ZZ Top from *Greatest Hits* (Warner Bros., 92).

The Gypsy Life
Words and music by John Gorka.

Blues Palace, 1992.
Introduced by John Gorka in *Temporary Road* (Windham Hill, 92).

H

Hail, Hail Rock 'n' Roll
Words and music by Garland Jeffreys.
Black and White Alike Inc., 1991.
Introduced by Garland Jeffreys in *Don't Call Me Buckwheat* (RCA, 91).

Happy Birthday to Me
Words and music by David Lowery.
Biscuits and Gravy Music, 1992.
Introduced by Cracker on *Cracker* (Virgin, 92). First effort from founder of the defunct Camper Van Beethoven.

Harry's Game (Irish)
Words and music by Padraig Brennan.
Television Music Ltd. (England), England, 1992.
Introduced by Clannad in the film and soundtrack LP *Patriot Games* (MCA, 92). Later came to popular attention in a Volkswagon commercial. Featured on the album *Anam* (Atlantic, 92).

Have You Ever Needed Someone So Bad (English)
Words and music by Phil Collen, Joe Elliott, and Robert John Lange.
Bludgeon Riffola, 1991/Zomba Enterprises, Inc., 1991.
Best-selling record by Def Leppard from *Adrenalize* (Mercury, 92).

Haven't Got a Clue (English)
Words and music by John Easdale.
Longitude Music, 1991/Binky Music, 1991.
Introduced by Dramarama on *Vinyl* (Chameleon, 92).

Hazard
Words and music by Richard Marx.
Chi-Boy, 1991.
Best-selling record by Richard Marx from *Rush Street* (Capitol, 91).

Hazy Shade of Criminal
Words and music by Carlton Ridenhour, William Drayton, Stuart
  Robertz, and Gary G. Wiz, words and music by The JBL.
Def American Songs, 1992/Bring the Noize Music, 1992.
Introduced by Public Enemy on *Greatest Misses* (Chaos, 92).

He Thinks He'll Keep Her
Words and music by Mary Chapin Carpenter and Don Schlitz.
EMI-April Music Inc., 1992/Getarealjob Music, 1992/Don Schlitz
  Music, 1992/Almo Music Corp., 1992.
Introduced by Mary Chapin Carpenter on *Come On, Come On*
  (Columbia, 92). Thoughtful lament on the progress of the battle
  between the sexes.

Heart of a Hero
Words and music by Luther Vandross.
EMI-April Music Inc., 1992/Uncle Ronnie's Music Co., Inc.,
  1992/Burbank Plaza, 1992.
Introduced by Luther Vandross in the film *Hero* (92).

Here I Go Again
Words and music by Glenn Jones.
Luella Music, 1992.
Best-selling record by Glenn Jones from *Here I Go Again* (Atlantic,
  92).

Hey Mister (I Need This Job)
Words and music by Kerry Chater and Renee Armand.
Careers-BMG, 1992/Padre Hotel Music, 1992/Willesden Music, Inc.,
  1992.
Introduced by Shenandoah on *Long Time Comin'* (MCA, 92). Taking
  on the realities of the recession, country style.

High (English)
Words and music by Robert Smith, Simon Gallup, Boris Williams,
  Purl Thompson, and Perry Bamonte.
Fiction Songs U.S. Inc., 1992.
Best-selling record by The Cure from *Wish* (Elektra Fiction, 92).

Hit (Icelandic)
English words and music by The Sugarcubes.
Virgin Music, Inc., 1991.
Best-selling record by The Sugarcubes from *Stick Around for Joy*
  (Elektra, 92).

Hold on My Heart (English)
Words and music by Anthony Banks, Phil Collins, and Mike
  Rutherford.

Anthony Banks, England, 1991/Mike Rutherford, England,
   1991/Phil Collins, England, 1991/Hit & Run Music, 1991.
Best-selling record by Genesis from *We Can't Dance* (Atlantic, 91).

Honey Love
Words and music by Robert Kelly.
Willesden Music, Inc., 1992/R. Kelly Music, 1992.
Best-selling record by R. Kelly & Public Announcement from *Born
   into the '90s* (Jive, 92).

Hooked on the Memory of You
Words and music by Neil Diamond.
Stonebridge Music, 1991.
Introduced by Neil Diamond with Kim Carnes on *Lovescape*
   (Columbia, 91).

Hot Fun in the Summertime
Words and music by Sylvester Stewart.
Mijac Music, 1969.
Revived by The Beach Boys on *Back to Paradise* (Brother, 92).

Hotel Illness
Words and music by Chris Robinson and Rich Robinson.
Enough to Contend With, 1992.
Best-selling record by The Black Crowes from *The Southern Harmony
   & Musical Companion* (Def American/Reprise, 92).

How About That (English)
Words and music by Bones Howe and Terry Thomas.
Warner-Chappell Music, 1992/TJT, 1992/Phantom, 1992/WB Music
   Corp., 1992.
Best-selling record by Bad Company from *Here Comes Trouble*
   (Atlantic, 92).

How Do You Talk to an Angel
Words and music by Barry Coffing, Steve Tyrell, and Stephanie Tyrell.
Tyrell Music Group, 1992.
Best-selling record by The Heights from the TV show and soundtrack
   album *The Heights* (Capital, 92). Vocal by James Walters. Song's
   success did not prevent the show's welcome demise.

Human Touch
Words and music by Bruce Springsteen.
Bruce Springsteen Publishing, 1992.
Best-selling record by Bruce Springsteen from *Human Touch*
   (Columbia, 92). Nominated for a Grammy Award, Best Rock Song
   of the Year, 1992.

Humpin' Around
Words and music by L. A. Reid (pseudonym for Antonio Reid), Babyface (pseudonym for Kenny Edmunds), Daryl Simmons, Bobby Brown, and Stylz.
Kear Music, 1992/Green Skirt Music, 1992/MCA Music, 1992/Bobby Brown, 1992/Stylz Music, 1992.
Best-selling record by Bobby Brown from *Bobby* (MCA, 92).

I

I Am a Town
Words and music by Mary Chapin Carpenter.
EMI-April Music Inc., 1992/Getarealjob Music, 1992.
Mary Chapin Carpenter in *Come On, Come On* (Columbia, 92).

I Can't Dance (English)
Words and music by Anthony Banks, Phil Collins, and Mike
    Rutherford.
Mike Rutherford, England, 1991/Phil Collins, England,
    1991/Anteater Music, 1991/Hit & Run Music, 1991.
Best-selling record by Genesis from *We Can't Dance* (Atlantic, 91).

I Can't Make You Love Me
Words and music by Mike Reid and Allen Shamblin.
Almo Music Corp., 1991/Brio Blues, 1991/Hayes Street, 1991.
Best-selling record by Bonnie Raitt from *Luck of the Draw* (Capitol,
    91).

I Can't Stand the Rain
Words and music by Ann Peebles, Donald Bryant, and Bernard
    Miller.
Burlington Music Corp., 1974.
Revived by Ann Peebles on *Full-Time Love* (Bullseye Blues, 92).

I Could Use a Little Love (Right Now)
Words and music by Barry Eastmond and Jolyann Skinner.
WB Music Corp., 1992/Heritage Hill Music, 1992/Zomba
    Enterprises, Inc., 1992/Jo Skin, 1992.
Best-selling record by Ralph Tresvant from *Time for Love* (Capital,
    92).

I Cross My Heart
Words and music by Steve Dorff and Eric Kaz.

Warner-Elektra-Asylum Music Inc., 1992/Dorff Songs, 1992/Zena
Music, 1992.
Best-selling record by George Strait from the film and soundtrack LP
Pure Country.

I Don't Sleep, I Drink Coffee Instead
Words and music by Brenda Kahn.
Through Being Cool Music, 1991/Warner-Tamerlane Publishing
Corp., 1991.
Introduced by Brenda Kahn on *Epiphany in Brooklyn* (Chaos, 92). A
throwback beat chanteuse in the Rickie Lee Jones/Laura Nyro
mode.

I Feel Lucky
Words and music by Mary Chapin Carpenter and Don Schlitz.
EMI-April Music Inc., 1992/Getarealjob Music, 1992/Don Schlitz
Music, 1992/Almo Music Corp., 1992.
Best-selling record by Mary Chapin Carpenter from *Come On, Come
On* (Columbia, 92). Nominated for a Grammy Award, Best Country
Song of the Year, 1992.

I Got a Thang 4 Ya!
Words and music by Tony Tolbert and Lance Alexander.
New Perspective Publishing, Inc., 1992.
Best-selling record by Lo-Key from *Where Dey At?* (Perspective, 92).

I Got My Education
Words and music by Orville Brimsley Evans and David Cole.
Class Clown Music, 1992.
Introduced by Uncanny Alliance (A & M, 92).

I Have Nothing
Music by David Foster, words by Linda Thompson.
Warner-Tamerlane Publishing Corp., 1992/One Four Three,
1992/Linda's Boys Music, 1992.
Introduced by Whitney Houston in the film and soundtrack LP *The
Bodyguard* (Arista, 92). Nominated for an Academy Award, Best
Song of the Year, 1992.

I Love You Period
Words and music by Terry Anderson.
Slow Train Music, 1992/Trailer Trash Music, 1992/BMG Songs Inc.,
1992.
Introduced by Dan Baird in *Love Songs for the Hearing Impaired* (Def
American, 92).

I Love Your Smile
Words and music by Narada Michael Walden, Shanice Wilson,
    Sylvester Jackson, and Jarvis LaRue Baker.
Shanice 4U, 1991/Gratitude Sky Music, Inc., 1991.
Best-selling record by Shanice from *Inner Child* (Motown, 91).

I Saw the Light
Words and music by Lisa Angelle and Andrew Gold.
Great Eastern Music, 1992/Sluggo Songs, 1992/Sister Elisabeth
    Music, 1992.
Best-selling record by Wynonna from *Wynonna* (Curb, 92).

I Still Believe in You
Words and music by Vince Gill and John Jarvis.
Benefit, 1992/Inspector Barlow, 1992/Bug Music, 1992.
Best-selling record by Vince Gill from *I Never Knew Lonely* (RCA, 92).
    Won a Grammy Award, and Best Country Song of the Year, 1992.

I Wanna Love You
Words and music by Vassal Benford and Ron Spearman.
WB Music Corp., 1992/Gradington Music, 1992/MCA Music,
    1992/Warner-Tamerlane Publishing Corp., 1992/Music Corp. of
    America, 1992.
Best-selling record by Jade from the film and soundtrack LP *Class Act*
    (Giant, 92).

I Will Always Love You
Words and music by Dolly Parton.
Velvet Apple Music, 1973.
Best-selling record by Whitney Houston from the film and soundtrack
    of *The Bodyguard* (Arista, 92). Also performed in the film by John
    Doe, who put out a single (Warner Bros, 92).

I Will Be Here for You
Words and music by Michael W. Smith and Diane Warren.
O'Ryan Music, Inc, 1991/Reunion, 1991/Realsongs, 1991.
Best-selling record by Michael W. Smith from *Change Your World*
    (Reunion/Geffen, 92).

I Will Follow Him (French)
English words by Norman Gimbel, French words by Jacques Plante,
    music by Arthur Altman, J. W. Stole, and Del Roma.
Leeds Music Corp., 1962.
Performed in the film and on soundtrack LP *Sister Act* (Hollywood,
    92).

I Will Remember You
Words and music by Amy Grant, Gary Chapman, and Keith Thomas.

Age to Age, 1991/Riverstone, 1991/Edward Grant, 1991/Yellow
  Elephant, 1991/Reunion, 1991.
Best-selling record by Amy Grant from *Heart in Motion* (A & M, 91).

I Wonder How She Knows (English)
Words and music by Elvis Costello.
Plangent Visions Music, Inc., London, England, 1992.
Introduced by Charles Brown on *Someone to Love* (Bullseye Blues, 92).
  Premier bluesman meets the prolific Brit.

I'd Die without You
Words and music by Attrel Cordes.
MCA Music, 1992.
Best-selling record by P.M. Dawn from the film and soundtrack LP
  Boomerang (Gee Street/LaFace , 92).

If I Didn't Have You
Words and music by Skip Ewing and Max D. Barnes.
Acuff Rose Opryland, 1992/Irving Music Inc., 1992/Hardscratch
  Music, 1992.
Best-selling record by Randy Travis from *Greatest Hits, Vol. 1* (Warner
  Bros, 92).

If I Ever Fall in Love
Words and music by Carl Martin.
Gasoline Alley Music, 1992.
Best-selling record by Shai from *If I Ever Fall in Love* (Gasoline Alley,
  92).

If I Lose Them
Words and music by Ron Shelton and Bennie Wallace.
Fox Film Music Corp., 1992.
Introduced by Aretha Franklin in the film and soundtrack LP *White
  Men Can't Jump* (EMI, 92).

If There Hadn't Been You
Words and music by Tom Shapiro and Ronald Hellard.
Edge o' the Woods, 1991/Kinetic Diamond, 1991/Moline Valley,
  1991/Careers-BMG, 1991.
Best-selling record by Billy Dean from *Billy Dean* (SBK, 91).

If You Asked Me To
Words and music by Diane Warren.
Realsongs, 1989/U/A, 1989/EMI-April Music Inc., 1989.
Best-selling record by Celine Dion from *Celine Dion* (Epic, 92).
  Previously a hit for Labelle.

If You Could See Me Now
Words and music by Tom Dean, Alana MacDonald, and Herb
Ludwig.
Hit List, 1992/Devon Square Music, 1992/Venutian Publishing Ltd,
1992/MDL Publishing, 1992.
Introduced by Devonsquare on *If You Could See Me Now* (Atlantic,
92).

If You Go Away
Words and music by Walter Afanasieff and John Bettis.
WB Music Corp., 1992/Wallyworld Music, 1992/John Bettis Music,
1992.
Best-selling record by NKOTB from *The Tour Collection* (Columbia,
92). Album is a foreign greatest hits repackaging of tunes by the
New Kids on the Block.

Ignoreland
Words and music by William Berry, Michael Stipe, Mike Mills, and
Peter Buck.
Night Garden Music, 1992/Unichappell Music Inc., 1992.
Introduced by R.E.M. on *Automatic for the People* (WB, 92).

I'll Be There
Words and music by Hal Davis, Berry Gordy, Willie Hutch, and Bob
West.
Jobete Music Co., Inc., 1970/Stone Diamond Music Corp., 1970.
Introduced by Mariah Carey on the TV show and in the album
Unplugged (Columbia, 92). Nominated for a Grammy Award, Best
Rhythm 'n' Blues Song of the Year, 1992.

I'll Remember You
Words and music by Bob Dylan.
Special Rider Music, 1992.
Performed by Grayson Hugh in the film and on the soundtrack of
Fried Green Tomatoes. Author is but a shadow of Bob Dylan in his
prime.

I'll Think of Something
Words and music by Jerry Foster and Bill Rice.
Polygram International, 1974.
Best-selling record by Mark Chesnutt from *Longnecks and Short
Stories* (MCA, 92).

I'm Breaking Down
Words and music by William Finn.

No publisher available.
Revived by Barbara Walsh in *Falsettos*. Introduced in 1979 in *In Trousers,* a previous musical by the author.

I'm in a Hurry (and Don't Know Why)
Words and music by Roger Murrah and Randy Van Warmer.
Murrah, 1992/Van Warmer Music, 1992.
Best-selling record by Alabama from *American Pride* (RCA, 92).

I'm Not Your Stepping Stone
Words and music by Tommy Boyce and Bobby Hart.
Screen Gems-EMI Music Inc., 1966.
Revived by The Sex Pistols in the film and soundtrack LP *The Great Rock 'n' Roll Swindle* (WB, 92).

I'm the One You Need
Words and music by Jody Watley, David Morales, and Alex Shartzis.
Rightsong Music Inc., 1992/Deb Mix Music, 1992/Alex Shartzis Music, 1992/EMI-April Music Inc., 1992.
Best-selling record by Jody Watley from *Affairs of the Heart* (MCA, 92).

I'm Too Sexy (English)
Words and music by Fred Fairbrass, Richard Fairbrass, and Rob Manzoli.
Hit & Run Music, 1991/Hidden Pun, 1991.
Best-selling record by Right Said Fred from *Right Said Fred* (Charisma, 92). One of the authors acted the part of a guitar player in a Bob Dylan video.

In a Lifetime (Irish)
Words and music by Padraig Brennan.
Television Music Ltd. (England), England, 1992.
Introduced by Clannad and Bono in the film *Patriot Games* (92). Featured on the album *Anam* (Atlantic, 92).

In a Sentimental Mood
Words and music by Duke Ellington.
Mills Music Inc., 1935/Famous Music Corp., 1935.
Revived by Billy Joel in the film and soundtrack LP *A League of Their Own* (Columbia, 92).

In My Life (English)
Words and music by John Lennon and Paul McCartney.
Northern Songs, Ltd., England, 1965/Music Corp. of America, 1965.
Revived by Bette Midler in the film and on the soundtrack LP *For the Boys* (Atlantic, 91).

In the Closet
Words and music by Michael Jackson and Teddy Riley.
Mijac Music, 1991/Warner-Tamerlane Publishing Corp.,
    1991/Donril Music, 1991/Zomba Enterprises, Inc., 1991.
Best-selling record by Michael Jackson from *Dangerous* (Epic, 91).

In the Still of the Night (I'll Remember)
Words and music by Fred Parris.
Llee Corp., 1956.
Revived by Boyz II Men in the TV show and on the soundtrack LP
    The Jacksons: An American Dream (Motown, 92).

In This Life
Words and music by Mike Reid and Allen Shamblin.
Almo Music Corp., 1992/Brio Blues, 1992/Hayes Street, 1992/Allen
    Shamblin Music, 1992.
Best-selling record by Collin Raye from *In This Life* (Epic, 92).

Insatiable
Words and music by Prince, words and music by New Power
    Generation.
Controversy Music, 1991/WB Music Corp., 1991.
Best-selling record by Prince & the New Power Generation from
    Diamonds and Pearls (Paisley Park, 91).

Inside
Words and music by Bill Morrissey.
Dry Fly Music, 1992/Bug Music, 1992.
Introduced by Bill Morrissey on *Inside* (Philo, 92). A duet with
    Suzanne Vega.

Into Tomorrow (English)
Words and music by Paul Weller.
NTV Music (England), England, 1992.
Introduced by Paul Weller in *Paul Weller* (Go Discs/London, 92).

Iron Lion Zion (Jamaican)
Words and music by Bob Marley.
Golden Rule Music, 1992/Cayman Music Inc., 1992.
Introduced by Bob Marley on *Songs of Freedom* (Island, 92). This
    previously unreleased demo of an undiscovered song was a hit when
    it was finally released in England.

Is It Good to You
Words and music by Teddy Riley and Tammy Lucas.
Zomba Enterprises, Inc., 1991/Donril Music, 1991.
Introduced by Teddy Riley, featuring Tammy Lucas, in the film and
    soundtrack LP *Juice* (MCA, 91).

Is There Life out There
Words and music by Susan Longacre and Rick Giles.
WBM, 1992/Long Acre Music, 1992/Edge o' the Woods,
    1992/Kinetic Diamond, 1992.
Best-selling record by Reba McEntire from *For My Broken Heart*
    (MCA, 92).

Is You Is or Is You Ain't My Baby
Words and music by Billy Austin and Louis Jordan.
Leeds Music Corp., 1944/MCA Music, 1944.
Revived by the cast in the musical and cast album of *Five Guys Named
    Moe* (Columbia, 92).

The Island (Irish)
Words and music by Paul Brady.
Almo Music Corp., 1992.
Introduced by Paul Brady on *Songs & Crazy Dreams* (Fontana, 92).

It Don't Bring You
Words and music by Mary Chapin Carpenter.
EMI-April Music Inc., 1992/Getarealjob Music, 1992.
Introduced by Maura O'Connell on *Blue Is the Colour of Hope*
    (Warner Bros., 92).

It's a Shame About Ray
Words and music by Evan Dando and Tom Morgan.
Dave & Darlene Music, 1992/Moo Music, 1992.
Introduced by The Lemonheads in *It's a Shame About Ray* (Atlantic,
    92). College cult question of the year: Who is Ray?

It's Probably Me (English)
Words and music by Sting, Eric Clapton, and Michael Kamen.
Magnetic, England, 1992/Blue Turtle, 1992/Warner-Tamerlane
    Publishing Corp., 1992.
Introduced by Sting, with Eric Clapton, in the film and soundtrack LP
    Lethal Weapon 3 (a & M, 92). Nominated for a Grammy Award,
    Best Song for a Movie or TV, 1992.

J

Jam
Words and music by Michael Jackson, Rene Moore, Bruce Swedien,
and Teddy Riley.
Mijac Music, 1992/Warner-Tamerlane Publishing Corp.,
1992/Donril Music, 1992/Zomba Enterprises, Inc., 1992.
Best-selling record by Michael Jackson from *Dangerous* (Epic, 92).

James Brown Is Dead
Words and music by Denzil Siemming.
BMG Songs Inc., 1991.
Introduced by L.A. Style (Watts, 91, Arista, 92)

Jeremy
Words and music by Eddie Vedder and Jeff Ament.
Innocent Bystander Music, 1991/Write Treatage Music, 1991.
Best-selling record by Pearl Jam in *Ten* (Epic, 91). Nominated for a
Grammy Award, Best Rock Song of the Year, 1992.

Jesus Built My Hotrod
Words and music by Ministry, words and music by Gabby Haynes.
Spurburn Music, 1992/Warner-Tamerlane Publishing Corp.,
1992/Latino Buggerveil Music, 1992.
Best-selling record by Ministry from the "symbol" album (Sire, 92).

Juice (Know the Ledge)
Words and music by Rakim (pseudonym for William Griffin).
EMI-Blackwood Music Inc., 1991/Eric B. & Rakim Music, 1991.
Introduced by Eric B. & Rakim in the film and soundtrack LP *Juice*
(MCA, 91).

A Jukebox with a Country Song
Words and music by Gene Nelson and Ronnie Samoset.

Warner-Tamerlane Publishing Corp., 1991/Mister Charlie Music, 1991/WB Music Corp., 1991/Samosonian Music, 1991.
Best-selling record by Doug Stone from *I Thought It Was You* (Epic, 91).

Jump
Words and music by Jermaine Dupri.
So So Def Music, 1992.
Best-selling record by Kriss Kross from *Totally Krossed Out* (Ruff House/Columbia, 92). The subteen duo evoked memories of Frankie Lymon & the Teenagers.

Jump Around (Irish)
Words and music by Larry Muggerud and Everlast Schrody.
T-Boy, 1992/Soul Assassins Music, 1992.
Best-selling record by House of Pain from *House of Pain* (Tommy Boy, 92).

Just Another Day
Words and music by Jon Secada and Miguel Morejon.
Estefan Music, 1992/Foreign Imported, 1992.
Best-selling record by Jon Secada from *Jon Secada* (SBK, 92).

Just Another Night
Words and music by Jude Cole.
Coleision, 1992/EMI-Blackwood Music Inc., 1992.
Introduced by Jude Cole on *Start the Car* (Reprise, 92).

Just Like a Man (Scottish)
Words and music by Justin Currie and Lain Hawie.
Polygram Music Publishing Inc., 1988/Polygram International, 1988.
Introduced by Del Amitri on *Change Everything* (A & M, 92).

Just Take My Heart
Words and music by Eric Martin, Andre Pessis, and Alex Call.
EMI-April Music Inc., 1991/Endless Frogs Music, 1991/Eric Martin Music, 1991/Bob-a-Lew Songs, 1991/Lew-Bob Music, 1991.
Best-selling record by Mr. Big from *Lean into It* (Atlantic, 91).

Justified and Ancient (English)
Words and music by Jimi Cauty, William Drummond, and Ricky Lyte.
E.G. Music, Inc., 1991/Warner-Chappell Music, 1991/WB Music Corp., 1991/BMG Songs Inc., 1991.
Best-selling record by The KLF (featuring Tammy Wynette) (Arista, 91).

K

Keep It Comin'
Words and music by Lionel Job, Joe Carter, Joseph Sayles, Dew
   Wyatt, Kev Scott, and Keith Sweat.
Harrindur Music, 1991/Joe Public Music, 1991/Keith Sweat,
   1991/E/A, 1991/WB Music Corp., 1991/Ensign Music Corp.,
   1991.
Best-selling record by Keith Sweat from *Keep It Comin'* (Elektra, 91).

Keep It Comin' (Dance Til You Can't No More)
Words and music by Robert Clivilles, David Cole, Anthony Quiles,
   and Duran Ramos.
Cole-Clivilles, 1992/Virgin Music, Inc., 1992.
Introduced by C & C Music Factory, featuring Q/Unique and
   Deborah Cooper, in the film and soundtrack LP *Buffy, the Vampire
   Slayer* (Columbia, 92).

Keep on Walkin'
Words and music by Steve Hurley, Marc Williams, and Kim Sims.
Last Song Music, 1991/Third Coast Music, 1991.
Best-selling record by Cece Penniston from *Finally* (A & M, 91).

L

Language of Violence
Words and music by Michael Franti and Mark Pistel.
Beat Nigs, 1992/Polygram International, 1992.
Introduced by The Disposable Heroes of Hiphoprisy in *Hypocrisy Is the Greatest Luxury* (4th & Broadway, 92).

Layla (English)
Words and music by Eric Clapton and Jim Gordon.
Stigwood Music Inc., 1970.
Revived by Eric Clapton on the TV show and album *Unplugged* (Duke/Reprise, 92). Won a Grammy Award, and Best Rock Song of the Year, 1992.

Let's Get Rocked (English)
Words and music by Phil Collen, Joe Elliott, Robert John Lange, and John Savage.
Zomba Enterprises, Inc., 1991.
Best-selling record by Def Leppard from *Adrenalize* (Mercury, 92).

The Letter
Words and music by Ed's Redeeming Qualities.
Ed's Quality Music, 1991.
Introduced by Ed's Redeeming Qualities on *It's All Good News* (Flying High, 91).

Life Is a Highway (Canadian)
Words and music by Tom Cochrane.
Falling Sky Music, 1992/BMG Songs Inc., 1992.
Best-selling record by Tom Cochrane from *Mad Mad World* (Capitol, 92).

Life Itself (English)
Words and music by George Harrison.

Zero Productions, 1992.
Introduced by George Harrison on *Songs by George Harrison 2* (Genesis Publications, 92). This previously unreleased tune comes from a book and record package, with illustrations by Keith West.

Light of a Clear Blue Morning
Words and music by Dolly Parton.
Holpic Music, 1992/Velvet Apple Music, 1992.
Introduced by Dolly Parton in the film and soundtrack LP *Straight Talk* (Hollywood, 92).

Lights of Louisianne
Words and music by Rob Muerer, Nancy Bacal, and Jennifer Warnes.
Warnes Music, 1992/Copyright Management Inc., 1992.
Introduced by Jennifer Warnes on *The Hunter* (Private Music, 92).

Like a Virgin
Words and music by Billy Steinberg and Tom Kelly.
Denise Barry Music, 1984/Billy Steinberg Music, 1984.
Revived by Big Daddy on *Cutting Their Own Groove* (Rhino, 91). This ingenious performance of the Madonna epic is set to the structure of Frankie Avalon's ode to a former generation's Goddess of Love, "Venus."

Little Angel, Little Brother
Words and music by Lucinda Williams.
Lucy Jones Music, 1992.
Introduced by Lucinda Williams on *Sweet Old World* (Chameleon, 92).

Little Miss Can't Be Wrong
Words and music by Chris Barron.
Sony Songs, 1991/Mow B' Jow Music, 1991.
Best-selling record by The Spin Doctors from *Pocket Full of Kryptonite* (Epic, 91).

Little Sister
Words and music by Lou Reed.
Oakfield Avenue Music Ltd., 1982/Screen Gems-EMI Music Inc., 1982.
Revived by Lou Reed on *Between Thought and Expression/The Lou Reed Anthology* (RCA, 92). Featured in the film *Get Crazy*.

Live and Learn
Words and music by Joe Carter, Joseph Sayles, Kev Scott, and Dew Wyatt.
Harrindur Music, 1992/Joe Public Music, 1992/Noiseneta Music, 1992/Ensign Music Corp., 1992.
Best-selling record by Joe Public from *Joe Public* (Columbia, 92).

Lord Have Mercy on the Working Man
Words and music by Kostas.
Songs of Polygram, 1992.
Best-selling record by Travis Tritt from *T-R-O-U-B-L-E* (WB, 92).

Lost
Words and music by Brenda Kahn.
Warner-Tamerlane Publishing Corp., 1992/Through Being Cool
    Music, 1992.
Introduced by Brenda Kahn on *Epiphany in Brooklyn* (Chaos, 92).
    Dedicated to the memory of Lou Reed's idol, poet Delmore
    Schwartz.

Louisiana Love Call
Words and music by Marty Grebb.
Step 3 Music, 1992.
Introduced by Maria Muldaur on *Louisiana Love Call* (Black Tie, 92).

Love (English)
Words and music by David Gavurin and Harriet Wheeler.
Geffen Music, 1992/Warner-Chappell Music, 1992.
Introduced by The Sundays on *Blind* (DGC/Geffen, 92).

Love Is on the Way
Words and music by Jason Bieler.
Love Tribe Music, 1992/MCA Music, 1992.
Best-selling record by Saigon Kick from *The Lizard* (Third Stone, 92).

Love Me
Words and music by Fil Brown and Tony Robinson.
Modern Science Music, 1990.
Best-selling record by Tracie Spencer from *Make the Difference*
    (Capitol, 90).

Love Me Tender
Words and music by Vera Matson and Elvis Presley.
Elvis Presley Music, Inc., 1956/R & H Music Co., 1956.
Revived by Amy Grant in the film and soundtrack LP *Honeymoon in
    Vegas* (Epic Soundtrax, 92).

Love of My Life
Words and music by Carly Simon.
C'est Music, 1991/TCF Music Publishing, 1991.
Introduced by Carly Simon on the film and soundtrack *This Is My Life*
    (Qwest, 92). Selected as this year's theme song for Mothers Against
    Drunk Driving.

Love Shoulda Brought You Home
Words and music by Bo Watson, Daryl Simmons, and Babyface
(pseudonym for Kenny Edmunds).
Saba Seven Music, 1992/Kear Music, 1992/Ensign Music Corp.,
1992/Green Skirt Music, 1992.
Best-selling record by Toni Braxton from the film and soundtrack LP
Boomerang (LaFace, 92).

Love Song for a Vampire (English)
Words and music by Annie Lennox.
BMG Songs Inc., 1992.
Introduced by Annie Lennox in the film and soundtrack LP *Bram
Stoker's Dracula* (Columbia, 92).

Love Theme from *Another World*
Words and music by David Lewis and Alicia Warren.
No publisher available.
Introduced by David Lewis and Alicia Warren on the TV show
Another World (92).

Love without Strings
Music by Jimmie Haskell, words by Carol Conners.
Hollywood Boulevard Music, 1991/Great Z's Music, 1991.
Introduced by Katrina Roth on the TV show *Morris the Cat presents: A
Salute to America's Pets* (91). Nominated for an Emmy award, 92.

Love You All My Lifetime (East German)
English words and music by Irmgard Klarmann and Felix Weber.
Arabella (Germany), Germany, 1992/BMG Songs Inc., 1992.
Best-selling record by Chaka Khan from *The Woman I Am* (Warner
Bros, 92).

Love's Got a Hold on You
Words and music by Keith Stegall and Carson Chamberlain.
Warner-Tamerlane Publishing Corp., 1991/Just Cuts Music,
1991/Patti Hurt Music, 1991.
Best-selling record by Alan Jackson from *Don't Rock the Jukebox*
(Arista, 91).

Low Self Opinion
Words and music by The Rollins Band.
Rok Godz, 1991/Imago Songs, 1991.
Introduced by The Rollins Band in *The End of Silence* (Imago, 91).

M

Magic and Loss
Words and music by Lou Reed.
Metal Machine Music, 1992/Screen Gems-EMI Music Inc., 1992.
Introduced by Lou Reed on *Magic and Loss* (Sire, 92). Dedicated to
the late Tin Pan Alley poet Doc Pomus.

The Majesty of Rock
Words and music by Derek Smalls, Dave St. Hubbins, and Nigel
Tufnell.
MCA Music, 1992/Discharge Music, 1992.
Introduced by Spinal Tap on *Break Like the Wind* (MCA, 92).

Make It Happen
Words and music by Mariah Carey, David Cole, and Robert Clivilles.
M. Carey Songs, 1991/Virgin Music, Inc., 1991/Cole-Clivilles,
1991/Sony Songs, 1991.
Best-selling record by Mariah Carey from *Emotions* (Columbia, 91).

Mama I'm Coming Home (English)
Words and music by Ozzy Osbourne, Zakk Wilde, and Lemmy
Kilmeister.
Virgin Music, Inc., 1991.
Best-selling record by Ozzy Osbourne from *No More Tears* (Epic, 91).

Mama Told Me Not to Come
Words and music by Randy Newman.
Unichappell Music Inc., 1966/Six Continents Music Publishing Inc.,
1966.
Revived by The Wolfgang Press in *Queer* (4AD, 92).

Masterpiece
Words and music by Kenny Nolan.
Kenny Nolan Publishing Co., 1992.
Best-selling record by Atlantic Starr from *Love Crazy* (Reprise, 92).

Maybe It Was Memphis
Words and music by Michael Anderson.
Atlantic Music Corp., 1991/First Release Music Publishing,
    1991/Cadillac Pink Music, 1991.
Best-selling record by Pam Tillis from *Put Yourself in My Place*
    (Arista, 91).

Midlife Crisis
Words and music by Faith No More.
Big Thrilling Music, 1992/Vomit God, 1992.
Best-selling record by Faith No More from *Angel Dust* (Island, 92).

Midnight in Montgomery
Words and music by Alan Jackson and Don Sampson.
Mattie Ruth, 1991/Seventh Son Music Inc., 1991/Golden Reed
    Music, 1991.
Best-selling record by Alan Jackson from *Don't Rock the Jukebox*
    (Arista, 91).

Mind of Love (Where's Your Head, Kathryn) (Canadian)
Words and music by k. d. lang and Ben Mink.
Bumstead (SOCAN), British Columbia, Canada, 1992/Zavion
    (SOCAN), British Columbia, Canada, 1992.
Introduced by k. d. lang on *Ingenue* (Warner Bros., 92).

Miserablism (English)
Words and music by Nick Tennant and Chris Lowe.
Virgin Music, Inc., 1991.
Introduced by The Pet Shop Boys on *Discography* (EMI, 91).

Miss Chatelaine (Canadian)
Words and music by k. d. lang and Ben Mink.
Bumstead (SOCAN), British Columbia, Canada, 1992/Zavion
    (SOCAN), British Columbia, Canada, 1992.
Introduced by k. d. lang on *Ingenue* (Warner Bros., 92).

Missing You Now
Words and music by Michael Bolton, Walter Afanasieff, and Diane
    Warren.
Warner-Chappell Music, 1991/Mr. Bolton's Music, 1991/Warner-
    Tamerlane Publishing Corp., 1991/WB Music Corp.,
    1991/Wallyworld Music, 1991/Realsongs, 1991.
Best-selling record by Michael Bolton from *Time, Love and Tenderness*
    (Columbia, 91).

Mr. Loverman (Jamaican)
Words and music by Rexton Gordon, Mikey Bennett, and H. Lindo.

Worldwide Anchor Music, 1992/Gunsmoke Music Publishers,
1992/Pow Wow Records, Inc., 1992.
Best-selling record by Shabba Ranks from the film and soundtrack LP
Deep Cover (Epic, 92).

Mr. Wendall
Words and music by Arrested Development.
EMI-Blackwood Music Inc., 1992/Arrested Development Music,
1992.
Best-selling record by Arrested Development from *3 Years, 5 Months &
2 Days in the Life Of...* (Chrysalis, 92).

Money Can't Buy You Love
Words and music by James Harris, III, Terry Lewis, and Ralph
Tresvant.
Flyte Tyme Tunes, 1992/Rated RT Music, 1992/Burbank Plaza,
1992.
Introduced by Ralph Tresvant in the film and soundtrack LP *Mo'
Money* (Perspective/A & M, 92).

Money Don't Matter Tonight
Words and music by Prince, words and music by New Power
Generation.
Controversy Music, 1991.
Best-selling record by Prince & the New Power Generation from
Diamonds and Pearls (Paisley Park, 91).

Mother
Words and music by Tori Amos.
Sword and Stone, 1991.
Introduced by Tori Amos on *Little Earthquakes* (Atlantic, 92).

Mouth for War
Words and music by Pantera.
Power Metal Music, 1992/Cota Music, 1992.
Introduced by Pantera on *A Vulgar Display of Power* (Atco, 92).

Move This (English)
Words and music by Manuela Kamosi and Jo Bogaert.
BMC, 1992/Bogam, 1992/Colgems-EMI Music Inc., 1992.
Best-selling record by Technotronic featuring Ya Kid K from *Pump
Up the Jam - The Album* (SBK/ERG, 92). Tune started out in life in
a Revlon TV commercial.

Mrs. Robinson
Words and music by Paul Simon.

Paul Simon Music, 1967.
Revived by The Lemonheads (Atlantic, 92). Included in the 25th
Anniversary package of *The Graduate* for which this originally
served as theme by Simon & Garfunkel.

My Beautiful Reward
Words and music by Bruce Springsteen.
Bruce Springsteen Publishing, 1992.
Introduced by Bruce Springsteen in *Lucky Town* (Columbia, 92).

My Evil Twin
Words and music by They Might Be Giants.
They Might Be Giants Music, 1992/WB Music Corp., 1992.
Introduced by They Might Be Giants on *Apollo 18* (Elektra, 92).

My Land
Words and music by Tim Robbins and David Robbins.
No publisher available.
Introduced by Tim Robbins in *Bob Roberts* (92).

My Lovin' (You're Never Gonna Get It)
Words and music by Thom McElroy and Denzil Foster.
Two Tuff-Enuff Publishing, 1992/Irving Music Inc., 1992.
Best-selling record by En Vogue from *Funky Divas of Soul* (East/West,
92). Nominated for a Grammy Award, Best Rhythm 'n' Blues Song
of the Year, 1992.

My Name Is Prince
Words and music by Prince and Tony M.
NRG Music, 1992.
Best-selling record by Prince & the New Power Generation from the
"symbol" album (Paisley Park, 92).

My Way (French)
English words and music by Paul Anka, French words and music by
Claude Francois.
E. Barclay-France, 1967/Juene Music-France, 1967/Management
Agency & Music Publishing, 1967.
Revived by Sid Vicious in the film and soundtrack LP *The Great Rock
'n' Roll Swindle* (WB, 92).

Mysterious Ways (Irish)
Words and music by U2.
Chappell & Co., Inc., 1991.
Best-selling record by U2 from *Achtung Baby* (Island, 91).

N

Nashville
Words and music by Amy Ray.
Virgin Songs, 1992/Godhap Music, 1992.
Introduced by the Indigo Girls in *Rites of Passage* (Epic, 92).

Neon Moon
Words and music by Ronnie Dunn.
Sony Tree, 1991.
Best-selling record by Brooks & Dunn from *Brand New Man* (Arista, 91).

New Fool
Words and music by Sidney Cox.
Sidney Lawrence Company, 1992.
Introduced by Alison Krauss & Union Station on *Every Time You Go Away* (Rounder, 92).

New Rose (English)
Words and music by Brian James.
Anglo Rock Music, 1977/Rock Music, 1977.
Revived by Gumball on *Wisconsin Hayride* (Columbia, 92). Introduced by The Damned.

No Man's Land
Words and music by Leon Russell and Bruce Hornsby.
Young Carny Music, 1991/WB Music Corp., 1991/Basically Zappo Music, 1991.
Introduced by Leon Russell on *Anything Can Happen* (Virgin, 92).

No One Can Forgive Me But My Baby
Words and music by Tom Waits.
Jalma, 1992.
Performed by John Hammond Jr. on *Got Love If You Want It* (Charisma/Pointblank, 92).

No One Else on Earth
Words and music by Sam Lorber, Stuart Harris, and Jill Colucci.
Sony Tunes, 1992/EMI Golden Torch Music, 1992/Heart Street,
    1992/Sony Tree, 1992/Edisto Sound, 1992.
Best-selling record by Wynonna from *Wynonna* (Curb, 92).

No Ordinary Love (English)
Words and music by Sade Adu and Stuart Matthewman.
Angel Music Ltd., 1992/Silver Angel Music Inc., 1992/Playhard
    Music, 1992.
Introduced by Sade in *Love Deluxe* (Epic, 92).

Norma Jean Riley
Words and music by Monty Powell, Dan Truman, and Robert Honey.
Resaca Beach Music, 1991/Warner-Tamerlane Publishing Corp.,
    1991/Dan Truman Music, 1991/Studio B. Music, 1991/Mountain
    Green Music, 1991.
Best-selling record by Diamond Rio from *Diamond Rio* (Arista, 91).

Not Enough Time (Australian)
Words and music by John Farris and Michael Hutchence.
Polygram International, 1992.
Best-selling record by INXS from *Welcome to Wherever You Are*
    (Atlantic, 92).

Not the Only One (Irish)
Words and music by Paul Brady.
Almo Music Corp., 1991.
Best-selling record by Bonnie Raitt from *Luck of the Draw* (Capitol,
    91).

Nothing But My Broken Heart
Words and music by Diane Warren.
Realsongs, 1992.
Best-selling record by Celine Dion from *Celine Dion* (Epic, 92).

Nothing Else Matters
Words and music by James Hetfield and Lars Ulrich.
Creeping Death Music, 1991.
Best-selling record by Metallica from *Metallica* (Elektra, 91). A rare
    ballad from the noted thrashers.

Nothing Short of Dying
Words and music by Travis Tritt.
Sony Tree, 1991/Post Oak, 1991.
Best-selling record by Travis Tritt from *It's All About to Change*
    (Warner Bros, 91).

November Rain
Words and music by Axl Rose.
Guns N' Roses Music, 1991.
Best-selling record by Guns 'N' Roses from *Use Your Illusion I*
(Geffen, 91).

Now and Forever
Words and music by Carole King.
Lushmole, London, England, 1992/Avon Gate Music, 1992.
Introduced by Carole King in the film and soundtrack LP *A League of
Their Own* (Columbia, 92). Nominated for a Grammy Award, Best
Song for a Movie or TV, 1992.

O

On 10 Square Miles of the Potomac
Words by Alan Jay Lerner, music by Leonard Bernstein.
Amberson Enterprises Inc., 1976/Boosey & Hawkes Inc., 1976.
Revived by The Indiana University Opera Theatre in *1600
Pennsylvania Avenue* (92).

Once and Only Thing
Words and music by Michael John LaChiusa.
No publisher available.
Introduced by Nancy Ticotin in *A... My Name Is Still Alice* (92).

One (Irish)
Words and music by Bono, words and music by U2.
U2, 1991/Chappell & Co., Inc., 1991.
Best-selling record by U2 from *Achtung Baby* (Island, 91).

The One (English)
Words by Elton John, music by Bernie Taupin.
Big Pig Music, Ltd., London, England, 1992/Warner-Chappell
  Music, 1992.
Best-selling record by Elton John from *The One* (MCA, 92).

100%
Words and music by Sonic Youth.
Savage Conquest Music, 1992.
Best-selling record by Sonic Youth from *Dirty* (DGC, 92).

One More Day
Words and music by Hank Wolinski, Cyril Neville, Jr., and Gaynelle
  Neville.
The Night Rainbow Music, 1992/Tee Off Music, 1992/Slaughter
  Neville Music, 1992/Liryco's Music, 1992/Irving Music Inc., 1992.
Introduced by The Neville Brothers on *Family Groove* (A & M, 92).

One More Time
Music by Tom Snow, words by Dean Pitchford.
Snow Music, 1992/Pitchford, 1992/Triple Star, 1992.
Introduced by James Ingram in the film and soundtrack LP *Sarafina* (Quest, 92).

Our Lady of the Bronx
Words and music by Larry Kirwan.
Starry Plough Music, 1992.
Introduced by Black 47 on *Black 47* (SBK, 92).

P

Painted Ladies
Words and music by Douglas Bernstein and Denis Markell.
No publisher available.
Introduced by Cleo King, Nancy Ticotin and Laura Dean in *A... My Name Is Still Alice.*

Papa Loved Mama
Words and music by Kim Williams and Garth Brooks.
Sony Cross Keys Publishing Co. Inc., 1991/Major Bob Music, 1991.
Best-selling record by Garth Brooks from *Ropin' the Wind* (Liberty, 91).

Pass the Mic
Words and music by Beastie Boys, words and music by Mario Caldato, Jr.
Brooklyn Dust, 1991.
Introduced by The Beastie Boys in *Check Your Head* (Capitol, 92).

Passionate Kisses
Words and music by Lucinda Williams.
Luella Music, 1989.
Introduced by Mary Chapin Carpentr in *Come On, Come On* (Columbia, 92).

Past the Point of Rescue (Irish)
Words and music by Mick Hanley.
Beann Eadair (Ireland), Ireland, 1991/Stainless Music Group, 1991/Foreshadow Songs, Inc., 1991.
Best-selling record on Hal Ketchum from *Past the Point of Rescue* (Curb, 91).

Peace (Jamaican)
Words and music by Jimmy Cliff.

Lilbert Music (Jamaica), Jamaica, 1992.
Introduced by Jimmy Cliff on *Breakout* (JRS, 92).

A Penthouse Apartment
Words by Joel Paley, music by Melvin Laird.
No publisher available.
Introduced by Jo-Ann Baum in the musical *Ruthless.*

People Everyday
Words and music by Speech (pseudonym for Todd Thomas).
EMI-Blackwood Music Inc., 1992/Arrested Development Music, 1992.
Best-selling record by Arrested Development from *3 Years, 5 Months & 2 Days in the Life Of...* (Chrysalis, 92). A tribute to Sly Stone.

People in Love
Words and music by Loudon Wainwright.
Snowden Music, 1992.
Introduced by Loudon Wainwright on *History* (Charisma, 92).

Perfidia (Mexican)
Music by Alberto Dominquez, English words by Milton Leeds.
Peer International Corp., 1939.
Introduced by Linda Ronstadt in the film and soundtrack LP *The Mambo Kings* (Elektra, 92).

Picasso's Mandolin
Words and music by Guy Clark, Radney Foster, and Bill Lloyd.
EMI-April Music Inc., 1992/RMG Music, 1992/Muckleroy Music, 1992/Careers-BMG, 1992/Kung Fu Grip Music, 1992.
Introduced by Guy Clark on *Boats to Build* (Asylum American Explorer, 92).

Play with Toys (English)
Words and music by Michael Ivey.
Colored Folks Music, 1991.
Revived by Basehead on *Plays with Toys* (Imago, 92).

Please Don't Go
Words and music by Harry Casey and Richard Finch.
Harrick Music Inc., 1979/Longitude Music, 1979.
Revived by K.W.S. in *Please Don't Go* (London, 92).

The President Jefferson Sunday Luncheon Party March
Music by Alan Jay Lerner, words by Leonard Bernstein.
Amberson Enterprises Inc., 1976/Boosey & Hawkes Inc., 1976.
Revived by The Indiana University Opera Theatre in *1600 Pennsyivania Avenue* (92).

Prodigal Daughter
Words and music by Michelle Shocked.
Songs of Polygram, 1992.
Introduced by Michelle Shocked on *Arkansas Traveler* (Mercury, 92).

Professional Showbizness Comedy
Music by Lynn Ahrens, words by Steven Flaherty.
No publisher available.
Introduced by Andrea Martin in *My Favorite Year* (92).

Pushermen
Words and music by Curtis Mayfield.
Warner-Tamerlane Publishing Corp., 1972.
Revived by Curtis Mayfield on *Pimps, Players & Private Eyes* (Sire, 92).
  Introduced in the film *Superfly* (72).

Q

Quicksand & Lies
Words and music by Billy Payne and Craig Fuller.
Morgan Creek Music, 1992/Feat Music, 1992.
Introduced by Little Feat in the film and soundtrack LP *White Sands*
  (Morgan Creek, 92).

R

Raining down on Bleecker Street
Words and music by Tom Dean, Alana MacDonald, and Herb
  Ludwig.
Hit List, 1992/Devon Square Music, 1992/MDL Publishing,
  1992/Venutian Publishing Ltd, 1992.
Introduced by Devonsquare on *If You Could See Me Now* (Atlantic,
  92).

Read My Lips
Music by Don Was, words by George Bush.
No publisher available.
Introduced by *A Thousand Points of Night* (Polydor, 92). A novelty
  tune made up of sound bites from the then-president.

Ready for a Miracle
Words and music by Art Reynolds and Bunny Hull.
Ensign Music Corp., 1992/Brassheart Music, 1992.
Introduced by Patti Labelle in the film *A Leap of Faith* (92). Featuring
  Edwin Hawkins.

Real Cool World (English)
Words and music by David Bowie.
Ensign Music Corp., 1992/Tinterette Music, 1992.
Best-selling record by David Bowie in the film and soundtrack LP *Cool
  World* (Warner Bros, 92).

Real Love
Words and music by Mack Rooney and Mark Morales.
Music Corp. of America, 1992/Second Generation Rooney Tunes,
  1992.
Best-selling record by Mary J. Blige from *What's the 411?*
  (Uptown/MCA, 92).

Remedy
Words and music by Chris Robinson and Rich Robinson.
Enough to Contend With, 1992.
Best-selling record by The Black Crowes from *The Southern Harmony & Musical Companion* (Def American/Reprise, 92).

Remember the Time
Words and music by Teddy Riley, Michael Jackson, and Bernard Belle.
Donril Music, 1991/Zomba Enterprises, Inc., 1991/Mijac Music, 1991/Warner-Tamerlane Publishing Corp., 1991/WB Music Corp., 1991/B. Funk, 1991.
Best-selling record by Michael Jackson from *Dangerous* (Epic, 91).

Rest in Peace
Music by Nuno Bettencourt, words and music by Gary Cherone.
Color Me Blind Music, 1992/Funky Metal, 1992/Almo Music Corp., 1992.
Best-selling record by Extreme from *III Sides to Every Story* (A & M, 92).

Restless Heart
Words and music by Peter Cetera and Andy Hill.
PPC Songs, 1992/Pillarview, 1992/Chrysalis Music Corp., 1992.
Best-selling record by Peter Cetera from *World Falling Down* (WB, 92).

Revolution
Words and music by Speech (pseudonym for Todd Thomas).
Arrested Development Music, 1992/EMI-Blackwood Music Inc., 1992.
Introduced by Arrested Development in the film and on the soundtrack LP *Malcolm X* (Chrysalis/EMI, 92).

Rhythm Is a Dancer (English)
Words and music by Benito Benites, John Garrett, III, and Thea Austin.
Hanseatic Music, 1992/Songs of Logic, 1992/Intersong, USA Inc., 1992.
Best-selling record by Snap from *The Madman's Return* (Arista, 92).
Reached number one in several European countries.

The Right Kind of Love
Words and music by Tommy Faragher, Lottie Golden, and Robbie Nevil.

MCA Music, 1992/Matak Music, 1992/Madfly Music, 1992/Dresden China Music, 1992/WB Music Corp., 1992.
Best-selling record by Jeremy Jordan from the TV show and soundtrack LP *Beverly Hills 90210* (Giant, 92).

Right Now
Words and music by Van Halen.
Van Halen Music, 1991.
Best-selling record by Van Halen from *For Unlawful Carnal Knowledge* (Warner Bros, 91).

Right Now
Words and music by Al B. Sure and Kyle West.
Al B. Sure, 1992/Willarie, 1992/EMI-April Music Inc., 1992/Across 110th Street, 1992.
Best-selling record by Al B. Sure from *Sexy Versus* (Warner Bros, 92).

The River
Words and music by Victoria Shaw and Garth Brooks.
Gary Morris Music, 1991/Major Bob Music, 1991/Midsummer Music, 1991.
Best-selling record by Garth Brooks from *Ropin' the Wind* (Liberty, 91).

Rock My Baby
Words and music by Bill Spencer, Philip Whitley, and Curtis Wright.
WB Music Corp., 1992/Stroudavarious Music, 1992.
Best-selling record by Shenandoah from *Long Time Comin'* (RCA, 92).

Rock Out of That Rockin' Chair
Words and music by Ken Welch and Mitzie Welch.
No publisher available.
Introduced by Andrea Martin, Linda Wallem and Carol Burnett on *The Carol Burnett Show*. Nominated for an Emmy.

Rock You Gently
Words and music by Henry Gaffney and Gregory Abbott.
Grabbitt, 1992/Sea Foam Music Co., 1992.
Introduced by Jennifer Warnes on *The Hunter* (Private Music, 92).

Roll of the Dice
Words and music by Bruce Springsteen.
Bruce Springsteen Publishing, 1992.
Best-selling record by Bruce Springsteen from *Human Touch* (Columbia, 92).

Romeo & Juliet
Words and music by Oliver Leiber.

Virgin Music, Inc., 1992/Oliver Leiber Music, 1992.
Best-selling record by Stacy Earl (featuring the Wild Pair) from *Stacy Earl* (RCA, 92).

Rump Shaker
Words and music by Aquil Davidson, David Wynn, Markell Riley, Teddy Riley, and Anton Hollins.
EMI-April Music Inc., 1992/Abdul Rahman Music, 1992/D. Wynn Music, 1992/Zomba Enterprises, Inc., 1992.
Best-selling record by Wreckx-N-Effect from *Hard or Smooth* (MCA, 92).

Run to You
Music by Jud Friedman, words by Allan Rich.
Nelana Music, 1992/Music Corp. of America, 1992/Music by Candlelight, 1992/Peer-Southern Organization, 1992.
Introduced by Whitney Houston in the film and soundtrack *The Bodyguard* (Arista, 92). Nominated for an Academy Award, Best Song of the Year, 1992.

S

Sacred Ground
Words and music by Vernon Rust and Kix Brooks.
David N. Will, 1992/Sony Cross Keys Publishing Co. Inc., 1992.
Best-selling record by McBride & the Ride from *Sacred Ground*
(MCA, 92).

Sad New Day (English)
Words and music by Me Phi Me, words and music by Chris Cuben-
Tatum.
EMI-Blackwood Music Inc., 1992/It's Ceeceetee Music, 1992.
Introduced by Me Phi Me in *One* (RCA, 92).

The Sad Sound of the Wind
Words and music by Jules Shear.
Juters Publishing Co., 1991/Music Corp. of America, 1991.
Introduced by Jules Shear on *The Great Puzzle* (Polydor, 92).

Satellite of Love
Words and music by Lou Reed.
Oakfield Avenue Music Ltd., 1978/Screen Gems-EMI Music Inc.,
1978.
Revived by U2 on *One* (Island, 92).

Save the Best for Last
Words and music by Wendy Waldman, Jon Lind, and Phil Galdston.
Longitude Music, 1991/Moon & Stars Music, 1991/Virgin Music,
Inc., 1991/Big Mystique Music, 1991/Kazoom, 1991/Polygram
International, 1991.
Best-selling record by Vanessa Williams from *The Comfort Zone*
(Mercury, 91). Nominated for Grammy Awards, Record of the
Year, 1992, and Song of the Year, 1992.

Saving Forever for You
Words and music by Diane Warren.

Realsongs, 1992.
Best-selling record by Shanice from *Beverly Hills 90210* (Giant, 92).

Sax and Violins
Words and music by David Byrne.
Bleu Disque Music, 1991/Index Music, 1991/WB Music Corp., 1991.
Introduced by Talking Heads on the film and soundtrack LP *Until the End of the World* (WB, 91).

Scenario (English)
Words and music by A Tribe Called Quest.
Zomba Enterprises, Inc., 1991/Jazz Merchant Music, 1991/New School Music, 1991.
Best-selling record by A Tribe Called Quest from *Low End Theory* (Jive, 91).

School Me
Words and music by Gerald Levert and Edwin Nicholas.
Trycep Publishing Co., 1991/Ramal Music Co., 1991/Willesden Music, Inc., 1991.
Best-selling record by Gerald Levert from *Private Line* (Atco East West, 91).

Seasons
Words and music by Chris Cornell.
You Make Me Sick I Make Music, 1991.
IB Chris Cornell in the film and on the soundtrack LP *Singles* (Epic Soundtrax, 92).

Seminole Wind
Words and music by John Anderson.
Almo Music Corp., 1992/Holmes Creek Music, 1992.
Introduced by John Anderson on *Seminole Wind* (BNA, 92).

Sesame's Treet (Belgian)
English words and music by Joe Raposo.
EMI Waterford Music, 1970/Sesame Street Inc., 1970.
Best-selling record by Smart E's from *Sesame's Treet* (Pyro-Tech/Suburban Base, 92).

Sexual (Netherlands)
English words and music by Rob Bolland and Ferdi Bolland.
Bolland and Bolland (Netherlands), Netherlands, 1992.
Best-selling record by Goddess from *The Sexual Album* (Bybeat, 92).

Shake the Sugar Tree
Words and music by Chapin Hartford.

Sony Tree, 1992.
Best-selling record by Pam Tillis from *Homeward Looking Angel* (Arista, 92).

She Is His Only Need
Words and music by Dave Loggins.
MCA Music, 1992/Emerald River Music, 1992.
Best-selling record by Wynonna from *Wynonna* (Curb, 92). Nominated for a Grammy Award, Best Country Song of the Year, 1992.

She Runs Hot
Words and music by Ry Cooder, John Hiatt, Jim Keltner, and Nick Lowe.
Plangent Visions Music, Inc., London, England, 1992/Tonopah & Tidewater Music, 1992/Whistling Moon Traveler, 1992/Careers-BMG, 1992/Oooeee Music.
Introduced by Little Village on *Little Village* (Reprise, 92).

She's Got the Rhythm (and I Got the Blues)
Words and music by Alan Jackson and Randy Travis.
Mattie Ruth, 1992/Sometimes You Win, 1992/All Nations Music, 1992.
Best-selling record by Alan Jackson in *A Lot About Livin' (and a Little 'Bout Love)* (Arista, 92).

She's Mad
Words and music by David Byrne.
Index Music, 1991.
Best-selling record by David Byrne from *Uh-Oh* (Luaka Bop, Inc., 92).

She's Playin' Hard to Get (English)
Words and music by Timmy Allen and William Walton.
Zomba Enterprises, Inc., 1992/RHO Music, 1992.
Best-selling record by Hi-Five from *Keep It Goin' On* (Jive, 92).

Ships That Don't Come In
Words and music by Paul Nelson and Dave Gibson.
Warner-Tamerlane Publishing Corp., 1992/Maypop Music, 1992/Wild Country Music, 1992.
Introduced by Joe Diffie on *Regular Joe* (Epic, 92).

The Show Must Go On (English)
Words and music by Queen.
Queen Music Ltd., 1990/Beechwood Music Corp., 1990.
Revived by Queen on *Innuendo* (Hollywood, 92).

Shut 'Em Down
Words and music by Carlton Ridenhour, Stuart Robertz, Gary G.
    Wiz, and Cerwin Depper.
Def American Songs, 1991.
Introduced by Public Enemy on *Apocalypse, 91...The Enemy Strikes
    Black* (Def Jam/Columbia, 91).

Sidewalks of the City
Words and music by Lucinda Williams.
Lucy Jones Music, 1992.
Introduced by Lucinda Williams on *Sweet Old World* (Chameleon, 92).

Silent All These Years
Words and music by Tori Amos.
Sword and Stone, 1991.
Introduced by Tori Amos on *Little Earthquakes* (Atlantic, 92).

Six Blocks Away
Words and music by Lucinda Williams.
Lucy Jones Music, 1992.
Introduced by Lucinda Williams on *Sweet Old World* (Chameleon, 92).

16 Tons of Monkeys
Words and music by Tonio K. (pseudonym for Steve Krikorian) and
    Steve Schiff.
No publisher available.
Introduced by Tonio K. in the Oscar-nominated documentary *Session
    Man* (92).

The Sky Is Crying
Words and music by Elmore James, Clarence Lewis, and Morgan
    Robinson.
Longitude Music, 1960.
Revived by Stevie Ray Vaughan in *The Sky Is Crying* (Epic, 91).

Slow Dance (Hey Mr. DJ)
Words and music by Robert Kelly, Tyrone Blatcher, and Michael
    Jefferson.
Willesden Music, Inc., 1992/R. Kelly Music, 1992/Zomba
    Enterprises, Inc., 1992/310 Jammin', 1992.
Best-selling record by R. Kelly & Public Announcement from *Born
    into the '90s* (Jive, 92).

Slow Motion
Words and music by Color Me Badd, words and music by Howie
    Thompson.
Me Good, 1991/Howie Tee, 1991/Irving Music Inc., 1991.
Best-selling record by Color Me Badd from *C.M.B.* (Giant, 91).

Smells Like Teen Spirit
Words by Kurt Cobain, music by Nirvana.
Virgin Songs, 1991/End of Music, 1991.
Best-selling record by Nirvana from *Nevermind* (DGC, 91). Nominated
  for a Grammy Award, Best Rock Song of the Year, 1992.

So Much Like My Dad
Words and music by Chips Moman and Buddy Emmons.
Rightsong Music Inc., 1992/Chips Moman, 1992/Attadoo, 1992.
Best-selling record by George Strait from the film and soundtrack LP
  Pure Country (MCA, 92).

So Much Rain
Words and music by Craig Carnelia.
No publisher available.
Introduced by K. T. Sullivan in *A... My Name Is Still Alice.*

So What'cha Want
Words and music by Beastie Boys.
Brooklyn Dust, 1991.
Introduced by The Beastie Boys on *Check Your Head* (Capitol, 92).

Some Girls Do
Words and music by Mark Miller.
Zoo II Music, 1992.
Best-selling record by Sawyer Brown from *Dirt Road* (Curb, 92).

Some Kind of Trouble
Words and music by Mike Reid, Brent Maher, and Don Potter.
Almo Music Corp., 1991/Brio Blues, 1991/Welbeck Music Corp.,
  1991/Blue Quill Music, 1991/Sheep in Tow Music, 1991.
Best-selling record by Tanya Tucker from *What Do I Do with Me*
  (Liberty, 91).

Somebody Loves You Baby (You Know Who It Is)
Words and music by Walter Sigler and Eugene Curry.
Gamble-Huff Music, 1991/Henry SueMay Publishing Inc.,
  1991/Tajai Music, 1991/Mighty Three Music, 1991.
Best-selling record by Patti Labelle from *Burnin'* (MCA, 91).

Somebody to Shove
Words and music by Dave Pirner.
WB Music Corp., 1992/LFR Music, 1992.
Introduced by Soul Asylum on *Grave Dancers Union* (Columbia, 92).

Someday We'll All Be Free
Words and music by Donny Hathaway and Edward Howard.

WB Music Corp., 1978/Kumumba Music Publishers, 1978.
Revived by Aretha Franklin in the film *Malcolm X* and on the album *Music from Malcom X* (Quest/WB, 92).

Someone to Hold
Words and music by Mariah Carey, Walter Afanasieff, and Trey Lorenz.
M. Carey Songs, 1992/Sony Songs, 1992/WB Music Corp., 1992/Wallyworld Music, 1992.
Best-selling record by Trey Lorenz from *Trey Lorenz* (Epic, 92).

Something Good (English)
Words and music by Kate Bush, music by Jez Willis.
Kate Bush Music, Ltd., London, England, 1985.
Best-selling record by The Utah Saints from *Something Good* (London/PLG, 92). Based on samples from the Kate Bush song, "Cloudbusting."

Something He Can Feel, see **Giving Him Something He Can Feel.**

Sometimes Love Just Ain't Enough
Words and music by Patty Smyth and Glen Burtnik.
EMI-Blackwood Music Inc., 1992/Pink Smoke Music, 1992/WB Music Corp., 1992/Hampstead Heath Music Publishers Ltd., 1992/War Bride Music, 1992.
Best-selling record by Patty Smyth from *Patty Smyth* (RCA, 92). Duet with Don Henley.

Somewhere Other Than the Night
Words and music by Kent Blazy and Garth Brooks.
Sophie's Choice Music, 1992/Major Bob Music, 1992/No Fences Music, 1992.
Best-selling record by Garth Brooks from *The Chase* (Liberty, 92).

Spiritual High (State of Independence) (English)
Words and music by Vangelis, Jon Anderson, J. T. F. Hood, and Grant Showbiz.
WB Music Corp., 1992/Tough Knot Music, 1992/Spheric BV Music, 1992.
Performed by Moodswings, featuring Chrissie Hynde, in the film *Single White Female* the EP *Moodfood* (Arista, 92).

Split and Slide
Words and music by Butch Hancock.
Rain Light Music, 1992/Bug Music, 1992.
Performed by Butch Hancock on *No Two Alike,* a self-produced album (92).

Stay (English)
Words and music by DeVante Swing.
EMI-April Music Inc., 1991/Deswing Mob, 1991.
Best-selling record by Jodeci from *Forever My Lady* (Uptown, 91).

Stay (English)
Words and music by Siobhan Fahey, Marcella Detroit (pseudonym
    for Marcella Levy), and Dave Stewart.
EMI Music Publishing, Ltd., London, England, 1992/Polygram
    International, 1992/Careers-BMG, 1992.
Best-selling record by Shakespeare's Sister from *Hormonally Yours*
    (London, 92).

Steam (English)
Words and music by Peter Gabriel.
Real World Music, 1992/Pentagon Lipservice Music, 1992.
Best-selling record by Peter Gabriel from *Us* (Geffen, 92).

Steel Bars
Words and music by Michael Bolton and Bob Dylan.
Warner-Chappell Music, 1991/Mr. Bolton's Music, 1991/Warner-
    Tamerlane Publishing Corp., 1991/Special Rider Music, 1991.
Introduced by Michael Bolton on *Time, Love and Tenderness*
    (Columbia, 91).

Sticks and Stones
Words and music by Elbert West and Roger Dillon.
JMV Music Inc., 1991.
Best-selling record by Tracy Lawrence from *Sticks and Stones*
    (Atlantic, 91). Featured on the TV movie *In Sickness and in Health*
    (92).

Sting Me
Words and music by Chris Robinson and Rich Robinson.
Enough to Contend With, 1992.
Best-selling record by The Black Crowes from *The Southern Harmony
    & Musical Companion* (Def American/Reprise, 92).

Stones in the Road
Words and music by Mary Chapin Carpenter.
Getarealjob Music, 1992/EMI-April Music Inc., 1992.
Introduced by Joan Baez on *Play Me Backwards* (Virgin, 92).

Straight Talk
Words and music by Dolly Parton.
Holpic Music, 1992/Velvet Apple Music, 1992.
Introduced by Dolly Parton in the film and soundtrack LP *Straight
    Talk* (Hollywood, 92).

Straight Tequilla Night
Words and music by Kent Robbins and Deborah Hupp.
Irving Music Inc., 1992/Colter Bay Music, 1992/Dixie Stars Music, 1992.
Best-selling record by John Anderson from *Seminole Wind* (BNA, 92).

A Street Man Named Desire
Words and music by Bill McCorvey, Rich Alves, and Gary Harrison.
Great Cumberland Music, 1992/Flawfactor, 1992/Longitude Music, 1992/August Wind Music, 1992.
Best-selling record by Pirates of the Mississippi from *Walk the Plank* (Liberty, 92).

Success Has Made a Failure of Our Home
Words and music by Johnny Mullins.
Sure Fire Music Co., Inc., 1961.
Revived by Sinead O'Connor on *Am I Not Your Girl* (Ensign, 92).

Suck You Dry
Words and music by Mudhoney.
Better Than Your Music, 1992/Warner-Tamerlane Publishing Corp., 1992.
Introduced by Mudhoney on *Piece of Cake* (Reprise, 92).

Sunny Weather Lover
Music by Burt Bacharach, words by Hal David.
Casa David, 1990/New Hidden Valley Music Co., 1990.
Introduced by Dionne Warwick on *Friends Can Be Lovers* (Arista, 92).

The Sweater (Canadian)
Words and music by Meryn Cadell.
Intrepid Music Group (SOCAN), Ontario, Canada, 1992/Meryn Cadell (SOCAN), 1992.
Introduced by Meryn Cadell on *Angel Food for Thought* (Reprise, 92).

Sweet November
Words and music by Babyface (pseudonym for Kenny Edmunds).
Kear Music, 1992/Sony Epic/Solar, 1992.
Best-selling record by Troop from *Deepa* (Atlantic, 92).

Sweet Suzanne
Words and music by John Cougar Mellencamp.
Full Keel, 1991.
Introduced by The Buzzin' Cousins in the film and soundtrack LP of *Falling from Grace* (Mercury, 92).

The Sweetest Drop (English)
Words and music by Peter Murphy and Paul Statham.

MCA Music, 1992/Incomplete Music, 1992.
Best-selling record by Peter Murphy from *Holy Smoke* (RCA/Beggar's
Banquet, 92).

Symphony of Destruction
Words and music by Dave Mustaine.
Screen Gems-EMI Music Inc., 1992/Mustaine Music, 1992.
Introduced by Megadeth in *Countdown to Extinction* (Capitol, 92).

T

Take a Little Trip
Words and music by Ronnie Rogers and Mark Wright.
Maypop Music, 1991/Wild Country Music, 1991/EMI-Blackwood
  Music Inc., 1991/Wrightchild, 1991.
Best-selling record by Alabama from *Greatest Hits, Vol. 2* (RCA, 91).

Take a Look at the Guy
Words and music by Ron Wood.
WB Music Corp., 1974.
Revived by Izzy Stradlin & The JuJu Hounds on *Izzy Stradlin & The
  JuJu Hounds* (Geffen, 92). Originally recorded by Ron Wood on his
  album *I've Got My Own Record to Do.* Ron Wood guests on guitar
  and vocals.

Take This Heart
Words and music by Richard Marx.
Chi-Boy, 1991.
Best-selling record by Richard Marx from *Rush Street* (Capitol, 91).

Take Your Memory with You
Words and music by Vince Gill.
Benefit, 1992.
Best-selling record by Vince Gill from *Never Knew Lonely* (RCA, 92).

Tears in Heaven (English)
Words and music by Eric Clapton and Will Jennings.
United Lion Music Inc., 1991/Drumlin Ltd. (England), 1991.
Best-selling record by Eric Clapton from the film and soundtrack *Rush*
  (Reprise, 91). Won Grammy Awards. Nominated for a Grammy
  Award, Best song for a Movie or TV, 1992.

Teen Angst (What the World Needs Now)
Words and music by David Lowery.

Biscuits and Gravy Music, 1992.
Best-selling record by Cracker from *Cracker* (Virgin, 92).

Tell Me What You Want Me to Do
Words and music by Narada Michael Walden, Tevin Campbell, and
Sally Jo Dakota.
Gratitude Sky Music, Inc., 1991/Tevin Campbell Music, 1991.
Best-selling record by Tevin Campbell from *T.E.V.I.N.* (Qwest, 91).

Tennessee
Words and music by Speech (pseudonym for Todd Thomas) and
Aerle Taree.
Arrested Development Music, 1992/EMI-Blackwood Music Inc.,
1992.
Best-selling record by Arrested Development from *3 Years, 5 Months &
2 Days in the Life Of...* (Chrysalis, 92).

Testify
Words and music by Gary Hines, Jimmy Jam (pseudonym for James
Harris, III), and Terry Lewis.
Flyte Tyme Tunes, 1991.
Introduced by Sounds of Blackness in *Evolution of Gospel*
(Perspective/A & M, 91).

Thank You for Talkin' to Me Africa
Words and music by Sylvester Stewart.
Warner-Tamerlane Publishing Corp., 1972.
Revived by Miki Howard in *Femme Fatale* (Giant, 92).

That Train Don't Stop Here
Words and music by Cesar Rosas and Leroy Preston.
Ceros, 1991/Bug Music, 1991/Whiskey Drinkin' Music, 1991.
Introduced by Los Lobos on *Kiko* (Slash/Warner Bros, 92).

That Woman in the Mirror
Words by Mae Richard, music by Cheryl Hardwick.
No publisher available.
Introduced by Barbara Feldon in the musical *Cut the Ribbons* (92).

That's What Love Is For
Words and music by Michael Omartian, Mark Mueller, and Amy
Grant.
All Nations Music, 1991/Moo Maison, 1991/MCA Music, 1991/Age
to Age, 1991/Reunion, 1991.
Best-selling record by Amy Grant from *Heart in Motion* (A & M, 91).

There Ain't Nothin' Wrong with the Radio
Words and music by Aaron Tippin and Buddy Brock.

Acuff Rose Opryland, 1992.
Best-selling record by Aaron Tippin from *Read between the Lines* (RCA, 92).

There Goes the Neighborhood
Words and music by Ice-T and Ernie C.
Rhyme Syndicate, 1992/ERN Kneesea Music, 1992.
Introduced by Body Count from *Body Count* (Sire, 92).

These Are Days
Words and music by Natalie Merchant and Stephen Buck.
Christian Burial Music, 1992.
Best-selling record by 10,000 Maniacs from *Our Time in Eden* (Elektra, 92).

Thinkin' Back
Words and music by Color Me Badd, words and music by Hamza
  Lee and Troy Taylor.
Me Good, 1991/Azmah Eel, 1991/Nubian Beat Music, Inc.,
  1991/Kharatroy Music, 1991/Chrysalis Music Corp., 1991.
Best-selling record by Color Me Badd from *C.M.B.* (Giant, 91).

This Used to Be My Playground
Words and music by Madonna Ciccone and Shep Pettibone.
WB Music Corp., 1992/Bleu Disque Music, 1992/Webo Girl,
  1992/Shepsongs, 1992/MCA Music, 1992.
Best-selling record by Madonna from the film *A League of Their Own* (Sire, 92). Released on the album *Barcelona Gold* (WB, 92).

Thorn in My Pride
Words and music by Chris Robinson and Rich Robinson.
Enough to Contend With, 1992.
Best-selling record by The Black Crowes from *The Southern Harmony
  & Musical Companion* (Def American/Reprise, 92).

Thought I'd Died and Gone to Heaven
Words and music by Bryan Adams and Robert John Lange.
Almo Music Corp., 1991/Almimo Music, Inc., 1991/Zomba
  Enterprises, Inc., 1991.
Best-selling record by Bryan Adams from *Wakin' up the Neighborhood* (A & M, 91).

'Till You Come Back to Me
Words and music by Karyn White, Steve Harvey, and Valerie Davis.
Warner-Tamerlane Publishing Corp., 1992/Kings Kid, 1992/Faithful
  Werks Music, 1992/Mizmo Music, 1992/EMI-Blackwood Music
  Inc., 1992/Steve Harvey Music, 1992.
Introduced by Rachelle Ferrell in *Rachelle Ferrell* (Capitol, 92).

Times Are Changing Back
Words and music by Tim Robbins and David Robbins.
No publisher available.
Introduced by Tim Robbins in the film *Bob Roberts* (92).

The Tips of My Fingers
Words and music by Bill Anderson.
Sony Tree, 1991/Champion Music Corp., 1991.
Best-selling record by Steve Wariner from *I Am Ready* (Arista, 91).

To Be with You
Words and music by Eric Martin and David Grahame.
EMI-April Music Inc., 1991/Eric Martin Music, 1991/Dog Turner
    Music, 1991.
Best-selling record by Mr. Big from *Lean into It* (Atlantic, 91).

To Hang a Dream On (English)
Words and music by Richard Thompson.
Beeswing Music, 1992.
Introduced by Richard Thompson in the film and soundtrack LP *Sweet
    Talker* (Capitol, 92).

To Love Somebody (English)
Words and music by Robin Gibb, Barry Gibb, and Maurice Gibb.
Gibb Brothers Music, 1967/Careers-BMG, 1967.
Revived by Michael Bolton on *Timeless* (Columbia, 92).

Today's Lonely Fool
Words and music by Kenny Beard and Stan Paul Davis.
Golden Reed Music, 1991/Loggy Bayou Music, 1991.
Best-selling record by Tracy Lawrence from *Sticks and Stones*
    (Atlantic, 91).

Tomorrow (English)
Words and music by Morrissey and Alain Whyte.
Bona Relations Music, 1992.
Best-selling record by Morrissey from *Your Arsenal* (Sire, 92).

Too Funky (English)
Words and music by George Michael.
Morrison Leahy, England, 1991/Dick Leahy (England), England,
    1991/Chappell & Co., Inc., 1991.
Best-selling record by George Michael from the album *Red Hot and
    Dance* (Columbia, 92).

Too Much Passion
Words and music by Pat DiNizio.

Screen Gems-EMI Music Inc., 1991/Famous Monsters Music, 1991.
Best-selling record by The Smithereens on *Blow Up* (Capitol, 91).

Two Sparrows in a Hurricane
Words and music by Mark Allen Springer.
Murrah, 1992.
Best-selling record by Tanya Tucker from *Can't Run from Yourself* (Liberty, 92).

2001
Words and music by Melissa Etheridge.
MLE Music, 1992/Almo Music Corp., 1992.
Introduced by Melissa Etheridge on *Never Enough* (Island, 92).

U

Under the Bridge
Words and music by Anthony Kiedis, John Frusciante, Flea, and
  Charles Smith.
Moebetoblame Music, 1991/MSC International, 1991.
Best-selling record by The Red Hot Chili Peppers from *Blood Sugar
  Sex Magik* (Warner Bros, 91).

Unlikely Lovers
Words and music by William Finn.
No publisher available.
Revived by Stephen Bogardus, Michael Rupert, Carolee Carmello, and
  Heather MacRae in *Falsettos* (92).

Unsung
Words and music by Page Hamilton.
Warner-Tamerlane Publishing Corp., 1991/VER Music,
  1991/Headlift Music, 1991.
Introduced by Helmet on *Meantime* (Interscope, 92).

Uptown Anthem
Words and music by Vincent Brown, Anthony Criss, and Kier Gist.
Naughty, 1991.
Introduced by Naughty by Nature in the film and on the soundtrack
  LP *Juice* (MCA, 91).

Uuh Ahh
Words and music by Nathan Morris, Wanya Morris, and Michael
  Bivens.
Mike Ten, 1991/MCA Music, 1991/Biv Ten, 1991.
Best-selling record by Boys II Men from *Cooleyhighharmony* (Motown,
  91).

V

Vibeology
Words and music by Peter Lord, Sandra St. Victor, and V. Jeffrey
   Smith.
EMI-April Music Inc., 1991/Leo Sun, 1991/Maanami, 1991/EMI-
   Blackwood Music Inc., 1991/Vermal, 1991.
Best-selling record by Paula Abdul from *Spellbound* (Captive, 91).

Victim of the Ghetto
Words and music by Eric Johnson, Tony Joseph, and Rom.
Virgin Music, Inc., 1992/Rom Music, 1992/Black Doors Music,
   1992/Pecot Music, 1992/T.J. Music, 1992.
Best-selling record by The College Boyz from *Radio Fusion Radio*
   (Virgin, 92).

Viva Las Vegas
Music by Doc Pomus, words by Mort Shuman.
Elvis Presley Music, Inc., 1964/Williamson Music Inc., 1964.
Revived by ZZ Top in *Greatest Hits* (Warner Bros, 91).

W

Walking on Broken Glass (English)
Words and music by Annie Lennox.
La Lennoxa Music, 1992/BMG Songs Inc., 1992.
Best-selling record by Annie Lennox from *Diva* (Arista, 92).

War of Man
Words and music by Neil Young.
Silver Fiddle, 1992.
Introduced by Neil Young on *Harvest Moon* (Reprise, 92).

Warm It Up
Words and music by Jermaine Dupri and Toni C.
EMI-April Music Inc., 1992/So So Def Music, 1992/House of Fun
    Music, 1992.
Best-selling record by Kriss Kross from *Totally Krossed Out*
    (Ruffhouse, 92).

Watch Me
Words and music by Tom Shapiro and Gary Burr.
Great Cumberland Music, 1992/Diamond Struck Music, 1992/In the
    Air Music, 1992/MCA Music, 1992/Gary Burr Music, 1992.
Best-selling record by Lorrie Morgan from *Watch Me* (MCA, 92).

Watch the Birds
Words and music by Lonette McKee.
Booley Boo Boo Music, 1992.
Introduced by Lonette McKee on *Natural Love* (Columbia, 92).

The Way I Feel About You
Words and music by Karyn White, Bruce Sterling, Zach Harmon,
    and Christopher Troy.
Warner-Tamerlane Publishing Corp., 1991/Kings Kid, 1991/Writing
    Staff Music, 1991/Gimme Half Publishing, 1991/Welbeck Music

Corp., 1991/Leftover Soupped Music, 1991/ATV Music Corp., 1991.

Best-selling record by Karyn White from *Ritual of Love* (Warner Bros, 91).

We Are One
Words and music by Dan Seals.
Pink Pig Music, 1992.
Best-selling record by Dan Seals from *Walking the Wire* (WB, 92).

We Didn't Know
Words and music by Stevie Wonder.
Steveland Morris Music, 1991.
Introduced by Whitney Houston with Stevie Wonder on *I'm Your Baby Tonight* (Arista, 91).

We Got a Love Thang (English)
Words and music by Eric Miller, Jeremiah McAllister, and Chantay Savage.
Last Song Music, 1991/Third Coast Music, 1991.
Best-selling record by Cece Penniston from *Finally* (A & M, 91).

We Hate It When Our Friends Become Successful (English)
Words and music by Morrissey and Alain Whyte.
Bona Relations Music, 1992.
Introduced by Morrissey on *Your Arsenal* (Sire/Reprise, 92).

We Have Come to Learn
Music by Larry Grossman, words by Buz Kohan.
No publisher available.
Introduced by the children's choir in the TV show *The American Teacher Awards* (91). Nominated for an Emmy Award, 1992.

We Shall Be Free
Words and music by Garth Brooks and Stephanie Davis.
Major Bob Music, 1992/No Fences Music, 1992/EMI-Blackwood Music Inc., 1992/Beartooth Music, 1992.
Introduced by Garth Brooks in *The Chase* (Liberty, 92). Written in response to the Rodney King verdict in Los Angeles.

We Tell Ourselves
Words and music by Clint Black and Hayden Nicholas.
Howlin' Hits Music, 1992.
Best-selling record by Clint Black from *The Hard Way* (RCA, 92).

We Will Rock You (English)
Words and music by Brian May.

Queen Music Ltd., 1977/Beechwood Music Corp., 1977.
Revived by Warrant in the film and on the soundtrack LP Gladiator (Columbia, 92).

Weight of the World (English)
Words and music by Brian O'Doherty and Fred Velez.
Nocturnal Eclipse Music, 1992/Dyad Music, Ltd., 1992/Susan Street Music, 1992.
Introduced by Ringo Starr from *Time Takes Time* (Private Music, 92).

Weirdo (English)
Words and music by Charlatans U.K.
Warner-Chappell Music, 1992.
Best-selling record by The Charlatans U.K. from *Between 10th & 11th* (Beggars Banquet/BMG, 92).

Welcome to Brooklyn
Music by Lynn Ahrens, words by Steven Flaherty.
No publisher available.
Introduced by Lainie Karan in the musical *My Favorite Year* (92).

What a Good Boy (Canadian)
Words and music by Steven Page, music by Ed Robertson.
Treat Baker Music (SOCAN), Ontario, Canada, 1992.
Introduced by Barenaked Ladies on *Gordon* (Sire, 92).

What About Your Friends
Words and music by Dallas Austin and Lisa Lopes.
D.A.R.P. Music, 1992/Diva 1 Music, 1992/Pebbitone Music, 1992/Tizbiz Music, 1992.
Best-selling record by TLC from *Oooohhh...on the TLC Tip* (Laface, 92).

What Becomes of the Brokenhearted
Words and music by James Dean, Paul Riser, and William Weatherspoon.
Jobete Music Co., Inc., 1966/Stone Agate Music Corp., 1966.
Revived by Paul Young in the film and soundtrack of *Fried Green Tomatoes* (MCA, 91).

(Without You) What Do I Do with Me
Words and music by Royce Porter, David Lewis, and David Chamberlain.
Sony Cross Keys Publishing Co. Inc., 1991/Milene Music Co., 1991.
Best-selling record by Tanya Tucker from *What Do I Do with Me* (Capitol, 91).

What God Wants, Part I (English)
Words and music by Roger Waters.
Pink Floyd, London, England, 1992/Roger Waters Music, 1992.
Introduced by Roger Waters on *Amused to Death* (Columbia, 92).

What Kind of Fool Do You Think I Am
Words and music by Alan Carmichael and Gary Griffin.
Sheddhouse Music, 1992/Robinette Music, 1992/Polygram
    International, 1992.
Best-selling record by Lee Roy Parnell from *Love without Mercy*
    (Mercury, 92).

What She's Doing Now
Words and music by Pat Alger and Garth Brooks.
Bait and Beer, 1991/Forerunner, 1991/Major Bob Music,
    1991/Midsummer Music, 1991.
Best-selling record by Garth Brooks from *Ropin' the Wind* (Capitol,
    91).

What's Good
Words and music by Lou Reed.
Metal Machine Music, 1992/Screen Gems-EMI Music Inc., 1992.
Introduced by Lou Reed on *Magic and Loss* (Sire, 92).

Wheels
Words and music by Amanda McBroom.
No publisher available.
Introduced by Laura Dean in *A...My Name is Still Alice.*

When I Look in Your Eyes
Words and music by C. J. Snare and Bill Leverty.
Sony Tunes, 1992/Wocka Wocka, 1992.
Best-selling record by Firehouse from *Hold Your Fire* (Epic, 92).

When It Comes to You (English)
Words and music by Mark Knopfler.
Straitjacket Music, 1992/Almo Music Corp., 1992.
Best-selling record by John Anderson from *Seminole Wind* (BWA, 92).

When She Begins
Words and music by Mike Ness.
Rebel Waltz Music, 1992/Sony Tunes, 1992.
Introduced by Social Distortion from *Somewhere between Heaven and
    Hell* (Epic, 92).

When She Cries
Words and music by Marc Beeson and Sonny Lemaire.

EMI-April Music Inc., 1992/Son Mare, 1992.
Best-selling record by Restless Heart from *Big Iron Horses* (RCA, 92).

Where You Goin' Now
Words and music by Tommy Shaw, Jack Blades, and Ted Nugent.
Ranch Rock, 1992/Warner-Tamerlane Publishing Corp.,
　　1992/Tranquility Base Songs, 1992/WB Music Corp.,
　　1992/Broadhead, 1992.
Best-selling record by Damn Yankees from *Don't Tread on Me*
　　(Warner Bros, 92).

Where's Johnny
Words and music by James McMurtry.
Short Trip Music, 1992/Bug Music, 1992.
Introduced by James McMurtry on *Candyland* (Columbia, 92).

Where's My Daddy
Words and music by Bemshi.
Music Corp. of America, 1992/Ascension Music, 1992/Bemshi
　　Music, 1992.
Introduced by Bemshi (Capitol, 92).

The Whiskey Ain't Workin'
Words and music by Ronnie Scaife and Marty Stuart.
Songs of Polygram, 1991/Partner, 1991.
Best-selling record by Travis Tritt with Marty Stuart from *It's All
　　About to Change* (Warner Bros, 91).

Whistle down the Wind
Words and music by Tom Waits.
Jalma, 1992.
Introduced by Tom Waits on *Bone Machine* (Island, 92). Dedicated to
　　the memory of Tom Jans.

White Men Can't Jump
Words and music by Dallas Austin and Ronnie Ran.
D.A.R.P. Music, 1992/Diva 1 Music, 1992.
Introduced by Riff in the film and on the soundtrack LP *White Men
　　Can't Jump* (SBK, 92).

Whoa!
Words and music by The Aquanettas.
Prize Pagoda Music, 1992.
Introduced by The Aquanettas (Major Label, 92).

A Whole New World
Music by Alan Menken, words by Tim Rice.

Wonderland Music Co., Inc., 1992/Walt Disney Music Co., 1992.
Best-selling record by Peabo Bryson and Regina Belle in the film and soundtrack of *Aladdin* (Disney, 92). Won an Academy Award, and Best Original Song for a Movie, 1992.

Who's Lovin' Who
Words and music by Smokey Robinson.
Jobete Music Co., Inc., 1971.
Jackson 5 song revived by the cast of *The Jacksons: An American Dream* (92). Album based on the TV special.

Why (English)
Words and music by Annie Lennox.
La Lennoxa Music, 1992/BMG Songs Inc., 1992.
Introduced by Annie Lennox in *Diva* (Arista, 92).

Why Do I Lie
Words by Dennis Spiegel, music by Curt Sobel.
T-L Music, 1992/Curt Sobel Music, 1992/Spiegel Music, 1992.
Introduced by the voice of Darlene Koldenhoven in the TV movie *Cast a Deadly Spell.* Winner of an Emmy for Best Song.

Why Me Baby
Words and music by James Todd, Teddy Riley, and Keith Sweat.
Keith Sweat, 1991/E/A, 1991/WB Music Corp., 1991/Donril Music, 1991/Zomba Enterprises, Inc., 1991/L.L. Cool J Music, 1991/Def Jam, 1991.
Best-selling record by Keith Sweat from *Keep It Comin'* (Elektra, 91).

Wicked
Words and music by Ice Cube.
Rhyme Syndicate, 1992.
Introduced by Body Count on *The Predator* (Warner Bros, 92).

Wicked As It Seems (English)
Words and music by Steve Jordan, Keith Richards, and Charlie Drayton.
Promopub BV, 1992/Warner-Tamerlane Publishing Corp., 1992/Risque Situe Music, 1992.
Introduced by Keith Richards on *Main Offender* (Virgin, 92).

Will You Marry Me
Words and music by Peter Lord, Sondra St. Victor, V. Jeffrey Smith, and Paula Abdul.
EMI-April Music Inc., 1991/Leo Sun, 1991/Maanami, 1991/PJA Music, 1991/EMI-Blackwood Music Inc., 1991/Vermal, 1991.
Best-selling record by Paula Abdul from *Spellbound* (Capture, 91).

Winter
Words and music by Tori Amos.
Sword and Stone, 1991.
Introduced by Tori Amos in *Little Earthquakes* (Atlantic, 92).

Wishing on a Star
Words and music by Billy Calvin.
May 12th Music Inc., 1978/Warner-Tamerlane Publishing Corp.,
    1978.
Revived by The Cover Girls from *Here It Is* (Epic, 92). Previously a hit
    for Rose Royce.

Wooly Bully
Words and music by Domingo Samudio.
Beckie Publishing Co., Inc., 1964.
Revived by The Smithereens in the film and soundtrack LP *Encino
Man* (Hollywood, 92).

Work to Do
Words and music by O'Kelly Isley, Ronald Isley, and Rudolph Isley.
Ronnie Runs Music, 1972/EMI-April Music Inc., 1972/Bovina
    Music, Inc., 1972.
Revived by Vanessa Williams on *The Comfort Zone* (Wing, 91).

Would
Words and music by Jerry Cantrell.
Buttnugget Publishing, 1992.
Introduced by Alice in Chains on *Dirt* (Columbia, 92).

Would I Lie to You
Words and music by Mike Leeson and Pete Vale.
Virgin Music, Inc., 1992.
Best-selling record by Charles & Eddie from *Duophonic* (Capitol, 91).

Wrong
Words and music by Lindsay Buckingham and Richard Dashut.
Now Sounds Music, 1992/Putz Tunes, 1992.
Introduced by Lindsay Buckingham on *Out of the Cradle* (Reprise, 92).

Y

You Can Depend on Me
Words and music by Ronnie Rogers and Jimmy Griffin.
Maypop Music, 1991/Wild Country Music, 1991/Careers-BMG, 1991.
Best-selling record by Restless Heart from *The Best of Restless Heart*
  (RCA, 91).

You Gotta Die Sometimes
Words and music by William Finn.
No publisher available.
Performed by Stephen Bogardus in *Falsettos* (92).

You Remind Me
Words and music by Dave Hall and Eric Militeer.
WB Music Corp., 1992/Stone Jam Music, 1992/Militeer Music, 1992.
Best-selling record by Mary J. Blige from the film and soundtrack LP
  Strictly Business (Uptown, 92).

You Showed Me
Words and music by Roger McGuinn and Gene Clark.
Tickson Music, 1965.
Revived by Salt 'n Pepa on *Blacks Magic* (Next Plateau, 91).

You Won't See Me Cry
Words and music by Wilson Phillips, words and music by Glen
  Ballard.
EMI-Blackwood Music Inc., 1992/Get Out Songs, 1992/Lentle
  Music, 1992/Smooshie Music, 1992/MCA Music,
  1992/Aerostation Corp., 1992.
Best-selling record by Wilson Phillips from *Shadows and Light* (SBK,
  92).

You're Invited But Your Friend Can't Come
Words and music by Tommy Shaw, Jack Blades, and Vince Neil.

Blondberry Music, 1992/Tranquility Base Songs, 1992/Holpic Music, 1992/Ranch Rock, 1992/Hollywood Pictures Music, 1992.
Best-selling record by Vince Neil from the film and soundtrack LP *Encino Man* (Hollywood, 92).

You've Been So Good up to Now
Words and music by Lyle Lovett.
Michael H. Goldsen, Inc., 1992/Lyle Lovett, 1992.
Introduced by Lyle Lovett on *Joshua Judges Ruth* (Curb/MCA, 92).

Lyricists & Composers
Index

Abbeloos, Olivier
  Anasthasia
Abbott, Gregory
  Rock You Gently
Abdul, Paula
  Will You Marry Me
Adams, Bryan
  Do I Have to Say the Words
  Thought I'd Died and Gone to
    Heaven
Adu, Sade
  No Ordinary Love
Afanasieff, Walter
  Can't Let Go
  If You Go Away
  Missing You Now
  Someone to Hold
Ahrens, Lynn
  Professional Showbizness Comedy
  Welcome to Brooklyn
Alexander, Lance
  I Got a Thang 4 Ya!
Alger, Pat
  What She's Doing Now
Alio, Joie
  Dizz Knee Land
Allen, Aaron
  Check out the Radio
Allen, Jeffrey
  Breakin' My Heart (Pretty Brown
    Eyes)
Allen, Timmy
  She's Playin' Hard to Get

Altman, Arthur
  I Will Follow Him
Alves, Rich
  A Street Man Named Desire
Ament, Jeff
  Jeremy
Amos, Tori
  Crucify
  Mother
  Silent All These Years
  Winter
Anderson, Bill
  The Tips of My Fingers
Anderson, John
  Seminole Wind
Anderson, Jon
  Spiritual High (State of Independence)
Anderson, Michael
  Maybe It Was Memphis
Anderson, Terry
  I Love You Period
Angelle, Lisa
  I Saw the Light
Anka, Paul
  My Way
Anthony, C. J.
  Games
The Aquanettas
  Whoa!
Armand, Renee
  Hey Mister (I Need This Job)
Arrested Development
  Mr. Wendall

101

Cordes, Attrel
  I'd Die without You
Cornell, Chris
  Seasons
Costello, Elvis
  I Wonder How She Knows
Cox, Pete
  Faithful
Cox, Sidney
  New Fool
Crane, Whitfield
  Everything About You
Creatore, Luigi
  Can't Help Falling in Love
Criss, Anthony
  Uptown Anthem
Cuben-Tatum, Chris
  Sad New Day
Currie, Justin
  Just Like a Man
Curry, Eugene
  Somebody Loves You Baby (You
    Know Who It Is)
D., Willie
  Clean up Man
Dakota, Sally Jo
  Tell Me What You Want Me to Do
Dando, Evan
  It's a Shame About Ray
Darnell, August
  Annie, I'm Not Your Daddy
Dashut, Richard
  Wrong
David, Hal
  Sunny Weather Lover
Davidson, Aquil
  Rump Shaker
Davis, Hal
  I'll Be There
Davis, Jesse Ed
  Baby Boom Che
Davis, Stan Paul
  Today's Lonely Fool
Davis, Stephanie
  We Shall Be Free
Davis, Valerie
  'Till You Come Back to Me

De Meyer, Patrick
  Anasthasia
Dean, James
  What Becomes of the Brokenhearted
Dean, Tom
  Bye Bye Route 66
  If You Could See Me Now
Dean, Tom
  Raining down on Bleecker Street
Depper, Cerwin
  Shut 'Em Down
Detroit, Marcella
  Stay
Devaney, Ian
  All Woman
Devoe, Ronnie
  The Best Things in Life Are Free
Diamond, Neil
  Hooked on the Memory of You
Dickson, Sean
  Divine Things
Dillon, Clifton
  Flex
Dillon, Roger
  Sticks and Stones
DiNizio, Pat
  Too Much Passion
Dinning, Dean
  All I Want
The D.O.C.
  Appetite for Destruction
Dominquez, Alberto
  Perfidia
Dorff, Steve
  I Cross My Heart
Drayton, Charlie
  Wicked As It Seems
Drayton, William
  Hazy Shade of Criminal
Dre, Dr.
  Appetite for Destruction
Drummie, Richard
  Faithful
Drummond, William
  Justified and Ancient
Dunn, Ronnie
  Boot Scootin' Boogie
  Neon Moon

Lyricists & Composers Index

Dupri, Jermaine
  Jump
  Warm It Up
Dylan, Bob
  I'll Remember You
  Steel Bars
Dylan, Jakob
  Ashes to Ashes
Easdale, John
  Haven't Got a Clue
Eastmond, Barry
  I Could Use a Little Love (Right Now)
Edmunds, Kenny see Babyface
Ed's Redeeming Qualities
  Christmas in Vermont
  The Letter
Eichstadt, Klaus
  Everything About You
Elfman, Danny
  Face to Face
Ellington, Duke
  In a Sentimental Mood
Elliott, Joe
  Have You Ever Needed Someone So Bad
  Let's Get Rocked
Ellis, Robert
  Dress
Emmons, Buddy
  So Much Like My Dad
Enya
  Caribbean Blue
Etheridge, Melissa
  Ain't It Heavy
  Dance without Sleeping
  2001
Etzioni, Marvin
  Can't Cry Hard Enough
Evans, Orville Brimsley
  I Got My Education
Ewing, Skip
  If I Didn't Have You
Fahey, Siobhan
  Stay
Fairbrass, Fred
  I'm Too Sexy

Fairbrass, Richard
  I'm Too Sexy
Faith No More
  Midlife Crisis
Faragher, Tommy
  The Right Kind of Love
Farris, John
  Not Enough Time
Finch, Richard
  Please Don't Go
Finn, William
  Father to Son
  I'm Breaking Down
  Unlikely Lovers
  You Gotta Die Sometimes
Fisher, Floyd
  Don't Be Afraid
Fisher, John Norwood
  Fight the Youth
Fisher, Philip
  Fight the Youth
Flaherty, Steven
  Professional Showbizness Comedy
  Welcome to Brooklyn
Flea
  Under the Bridge
Flowers, Danny
  Gulf Coast Highway
Foster, David
  I Have Nothing
Foster, Denzil
  Free Your Mind
  My Lovin' (You're Never Gonna Get It)
Foster, Jerry
  I'll Think of Something
Foster, Radney
  Picasso's Mandolin
Francois, Claude
  My Way
Franti, Michael
  Language of Violence
Friedman, Jud
  Run to You
Frusciante, John
  Under the Bridge
Fuller, Craig
  Quicksand & Lies

Harris, James, III see also Jam, Jimmy
  The Best Things in Life Are Free
  Forever Love
  Money Can't Buy You Love
Harris, Stuart
  No One Else on Earth
Harrison, Gary
  A Street Man Named Desire
Harrison, George
  Life Itself
Hart, Bobby
  I'm Not Your Stepping Stone
Hartford, Chapin
  Shake the Sugar Tree
Harvey, Polly Jean
  Dress
Harvey, Steve
  'Till You Come Back to Me
Haskell, Jimmie
  Love without Strings
Hathaway, Donny
  Someday We'll All Be Free
Hawie, Lain
  Just Like a Man
Hawkins, Sophie B.
  California Here I Come
  Damn, I Wish I Was Your Lover
Haynes, Gabby
  Jesus Built My Hotrod
Hellard, Ronald
  If There Hadn't Been You
Henderson, Luther
  Chicago Stomp
Hetfield, James
  Nothing Else Matters
Hiatt, John
  Don't Think About Her When
    You're Trying to Drive
  She Runs Hot
Hill, Andy
  Restless Heart
Hill, Byron
  Born Country
Hill, Dusty
  Gun Love
Himmelman, Peter
  Beneath the Damage & the Dust

Hines, Gary
  Testify
Hollins, Anton
  Rump Shaker
Honey, Robert
  Norma Jean Riley
Hood, J. T. F.
  Spiritual High (State of Independence)
Hooker, James
  Gulf Coast Highway
Horn, Trevor
  The Closing of the Year
Hornsby, Bruce
  Anything Can Happen
  No Man's Land
Howard, Edward
  Someday We'll All Be Free
Howard, Miki
  Cigarette Ashes on the Floor
Howe, Bones
  How About That
Hubbard, Gregg
  The Dirt Road
Hull, Bunny
  Ready for a Miracle
Humes, Lemel
  Ain't Nobody Like You
Hupp, Deborah
  Straight Tequilla Night
Hurley, Steve
  Keep on Walkin'
Hutch, Willie
  I'll Be There
Hutchence, Michael
  Not Enough Time
Ice Cube
  Wicked
Ice-T
  Cop Killer
  Freedom of Speech
  There Goes the Neighborhood
Isley, O'Kelly
  Work to Do
Isley, Ronald
  Work to Do
Isley, Rudolph
  Work to Do

Lyricists & Composers Index

Lyricists & Composers Index

Lyricists & Composers Index

Lyricists & Composers Index

Important Performances Index

Songs are listed under the works in which they were introduced or given significant renditions. The index is organized into major sections by performance medium: Album, Movie, Musical, Performer, Revue, Television Show.

Album

Achtung Baby
  Even Better Than the Real Thing
  Mysterious Ways
  One
Adrenalize
  Have You Ever Needed Someone So Bad
  Let's Get Rocked
Affairs of the Heart
  I'm the One You Need
Ain't I a Woman
  Ain't I a Woman
  Faithless World
AKA Graffiti Man
  Baby Boom Che
Aladdin
  Friend Like Me
  A Whole New World
All I Can Be
  Every Second
Am I Not Your Girl
  Success Has Made a Failure of Our Home
American Pride
  I'm in a Hurry (and Don't Know Why)

Amused to Death
  What God Wants, Part I
Anam
  Harry's Game
  In a Lifetime
Angel Dust
  Midlife Crisis
Angel Food for Thought
  Barbie
  The Sweater
Anything Can Happen
  Anything Can Happen
  No Man's Land
Apocalypse, 91...The Enemy Strikes Black
  Shut 'Em Down
Apollo 18
  My Evil Twin
Arkansas Traveler
  Prodigal Daughter
As Ugly As They Wanna Be
  Everything About You
Athens Andover
  Crazy Annie
Automatic for the People
  Drive
  Ignoreland

121

Until the End of the World
  Calling All Angels
  Sax and Violins
Us
  Digging the Dirt
  Steam
Use Your Illusion I
  November Rain
Vagabond Heart
  Broken Arrow
Vinyl
  Haven't Got a Clue
A Vulgar Display of Power
  Mouth for War
Wakin' up the Neighborhood
  Do I Have to Say the Words
  Thought I'd Died and Gone to
    Heaven
Walk the Plank
  A Street Man Named Desire
Walking the Wire
  We Are One
Wallflowers
  Ashes to Ashes
Watch Me
  Watch Me
Wayne's World
  Bohemian Rhapsody
We Can't Dance
  Hold on My Heart
  I Can't Dance
Welcome to Wherever You Are
  Not Enough Time
What Do I Do with Me
  Some Kind of Trouble
  (Without You) What Do I Do with
    Me
What's the 411?
  Real Love
When October Goes
  Are You Happy Now
Whenever We Wanted
  Again Tonight
Where Dey At?
  I Got a Thang 4 Ya!
White Men Can't Jump
  If I Lose Them
  White Men Can't Jump

White Sands
  Quicksand & Lies
The Williams Brothers
  Can't Cry Hard Enough
Wisconsin Hayride
  New Rose
Wish
  Friday I'm in Love
  High
The Woman I Am
  Love You All My Lifetime
World Falling Down
  Restless Heart
Wynonna
  I Saw the Light
  No One Else on Earth
  She Is His Only Need
You Gotta Pay the Band
  Bird Alone
Your Arsenal
  Tomorrow
  We Hate It When Our Friends
    Become Successful

Movie

Aladdin
  Friend Like Me
  A Whole New World
Batman Returns
  Face to Face
Beauty and the Beast
  Beauty and the Beast
Bob Roberts
  My Land
  Times Are Changing Back
The Bodyguard
  I Have Nothing
  I Will Always Love You
  Run to You
Boomerang
  End of the Road
  Give U My Heart
  I'd Die without You
  Love Shoulda Brought You Home
Bram Stoker's Dracula
  Love Song for a Vampire

Wash, Martha
Carry On
Waters, Roger
What God Wants, Part I
Watley, Jody
I'm the One You Need
Weller, Paul
Into Tomorrow
Wendy & Lisa
The Closing of the Year
Westerberg, Paul
Dyslexic Heart
White, Karyn
The Way I Feel About You
Whitley, Chris
Big Sky Country
The Wild Pair
Romeo & Juliet
The Williams Brothers
Can't Cry Hard Enough
Williams, Lucinda
Little Angel, Little Brother
Sidewalks of the City
Six Blocks Away
Williams, Vanessa
The Comfort Zone
Save the Best for Last
Work to Do
Wilson Phillips
Flesh and Blood
You Won't See Me Cry
The Wolfgang Press
Mama Told Me Not to Come
Wonder, Stevie
We Didn't Know
Wreckx-N-Effect
Rump Shaker
Wynonna
I Saw the Light
No One Else on Earth
She Is His Only Need

XTC
The Ballad of Peter Pumpkinhead
Young, Neil
War of Man
Young, Paul
What Becomes of the Brokenhearted
ZZ Top
Gun Love
Viva Las Vegas

Television Show

The American Teacher Awards
We Have Come to Learn
Another World
Love Theme from *Another World*
Beverly Hills 90210
The Right Kind of Love
Saving Forever for You
The Carol Burnett Show
Rock Out of That Rockin' Chair
Cast a Deadly Spell
Why Do I Lie
The Heights
How Do You Talk to an Angel
The Jacksons: An American Dream
In the Still of the Night (I'll
Remember)
Morris the Cat presents: A Salute to
America's Pets
Love without Strings
The Summer Olympic Games
Amigos Para Siempre (Friends for
Life)
Unplugged (Mariah Carey)
I'll Be There
Unplugged (Eric Clapton)
Layla

Awards Index

A list of songs nominated for Academy Awards by the Academy of Motion Picture Arts and Sciences and Grammy Awards from the National Academy of Recording Arts and Sciences. Asterisks indicate the winners.

1992
Academy Award
  Friend Like Me
  I Have Nothing
  Run to You
  A Whole New World*
Grammy Award
  Achy Breaky Heart
  Aint 2 Proud 2 Beg
  Beautiful Maria of My Soul
  Beauty and the Beast
  Beauty and the Beast*
  Constant Craving
  Digging the Dirt
  End of the Road
  The Greatest Man I Never Knew

Human Touch
I Feel Lucky
I Still Believe in You*
I'll Be There
It's Probably Me
Jeremy
Layla*
My Lovin' (You're Never Gonna Get It)
Now and Forever
Save the Best for Last
She Is His Only Need
Smells Like Teen Spirit
Tears in Heaven*
Tears in Heaven

List of Publishers

A directory of publishers of the songs included in *Popular Music,* 1992. Publishers that are members of the American Society of Composers, Authors, and Publishers or whose catalogs are available under ASCAP license are indicated by the designation (ASCAP). Publishers that have granted performing rights to Broadcast Music, Inc., are designated by the notation (BMI). Publishers whose catalogs are represented by The Society of Composers, Authors and Music Publishers of Canada, are indicated by the designation (SOCAN).

The addresses were gleaned from a variety of sources, including ASCAP, BMI, SOCAN, and *Billboard* magazine. As in any volatile industry, many of the addresses may become outdated quickly. In the interim between the book's completion and its subsequent publication, some publishers may have been consolidated into others or changed hands. This is a fact of life long endured by the music business and its constituents. The data collected here, and throughout the book, are as accurate as such circumstances allow.

A

ABCDE Music (ASCAP)
  see Warner-Chappell Music

Abdul Rahman Music (ASCAP)
  see EMI Music Publishing, Ltd.

Ackee Music Inc. (ASCAP)
  see Island Music

Across 110th Street (ASCAP)
  c/o SBK Songs
  1290 Avenue of the Americas
  New York, New York 10104

Acuff Rose Opryland (BMI)
  65 Music Square West
  Nashville, Tennessee 37203

Acuff-Rose Publications Inc. (BMI)
  2510 Franklin Road
  Nashville, Tennessee 37204

Aerostation Corp. (ASCAP)
  16214 Morrison Street
  Encino, California 91436

Age to Age (ASCAP)
  Address Unavailable

Alfred Avenue Music (BMI)
  see Tree Publishing Co., Inc.

All Nations Music (ASCAP)
  8857 W. Blvd., Suite 200
  Beverly Hills, California 90210

145

List of Publishers

Almimo Music, Inc. (BMI)
1358 N La Brea
Los Angeles, California 90028

Almo Music Corp. (ASCAP)
1416 N. La Brea Avenue
Hollywood, California 90028

Amberson Enterprises Inc. (ASCAP)
see Boosey & Hawkes Inc.

Among Others Music (BMI)
see Warner-Chappell Music

Angel Music Ltd. (ASCAP)
P.O. Box 1276
Great Neck, New York 11024

Anglo Rock Music
Address Unavailable

Anteater Music (ASCAP)
c/o Bradshaw & Thomas
8607 Sherwood Drive
Los Angeles, California 90069

Arabella (Germany)
Address Unavailable

Arrested Development Music (BMI)
see EMI Music Publishing, Ltd.

Ascension Music (BMI)
14-29 212th Avenue
Bayside, New York 11360

Atlantic Music Corp. (BMI)
6124 Selma Avenue
Hollywood, California 90028

Attadoo (BMI)
c/o Bobby Emmons
Johnson Chapel Road
Brentwood, Tennessee 37027

ATV Music Corp. (BMI)
6363 Sunset Blvd
Los Angeles, California 90028

August Wind Music (BMI)
see Longitude Music

Aunt Hilda's Music (ASCAP)
see Zomba Enterprises, Inc.

Avant Garde Music (ASCAP)
9229 Sunset Blvd.,
Suite 813
Los Angeles, California 90069

Avon Gate Music (BMI)
see EMI Music Publishing, Ltd.

Azmah Eel (ASCAP)
see Me Good

B

B. Funk (ASCAP)
see Warner-Chappell Music

Badams (ASCAP)
see Almo Music Corp.

Bait and Beer (ASCAP)
c/o Terrell Tye
P.O. Box 120657
Nashville, Tennessee 37212

Denise Barry Music (ASCAP)
c/o Peter T. Paterno, Esq.
Manatt, Phelps, Rothenberg & Tunney
11355 W. Olympic Blvd.
Los Angeles, California 90064

Basically Zappo Music (ASCAP)
see Warner-Chappell Music

Beann Eadair (Ireland)
Address Unavailable

Beartooth Music (BMI)
see EMI Music Publishing, Ltd.

Beat Nigs (ASCAP)
see Polygram Music Publishing Inc.

Beckie Publishing Co., Inc. (BMI)
P.O. Box 14671
Memphis, Tennessee 38114

Beechwood Music Corp. (BMI)
6255 Sunset Blvd.
Hollywood, California 90028

Beeswing Music (BMI)
c/o Gary Stamler
2029 Century Park, E., Suite 1500
Los Angeles, California 90067

Beginner Music (ASCAP)
P.O. Box 2532
Muscle Shoals, Alabama 35662

Beledat Music (ASCAP)
see Flyte Tyme Tunes

Belwin-Mills Publishing Corp. (ASCAP)
1776 Broadway, 11th Fl.
New York, New York 10019

Bemshi Music (BMI)
160 Claremont Avenue
New York, New York 10027

Benefit (BMI)
Address Unavailable

Better Than Your Music (BMI)
see Warner-Chappell Music

John Bettis Music (ASCAP)
c/o Harley Williams
1900 Avenue of the Stars
Suite 1200
Los Angeles, California 90067

Big Giant Music (BMI)
see Warner-Chappell Music

Big Life Music (BMI)
see Warner-Chappell Music

Big Mystique Music (BMI)
see EMI Music Publishing, Ltd.

Big Thrilling Music (ASCAP)
see Of the Fire Music

Binky Music (BMI)
see Longitude Music

Biscuits and Gravy Music (BMI)
see Warner-Chappell Music

Biv Ten
see Diva One

Black and White Alike Inc. (ASCAP)
201 E. 28th Street
New York, New York 10016

Black Doors Music (ASCAP)
see EMI Music Publishing, Ltd.

Black Satin Music (BMI)
see Warner-Chappell Music

Blackhawk Music Co. (BMI)
1420 Marron Circle, N.E.
Albuquerque, New Mexico 87112

Bleu Disque Music (ASCAP)
c/o Warner Brothers Music
9000 Sunset Blvd., Penthouse
Los Angeles, California 90069

Blondberry Music (ASCAP)
see Warner-Chappell Music

Bludgeon Riffola (ASCAP)
Address Unavailable

Blue Midnight Music (ASCAP)
c/o Bug Music
6777 Hollywood Blvd., 9th Fl.
Hollywood, California 90028

Blue Quill Music (ASCAP)
see Cherry Lane Music Co., Inc.

Blue Saint Music (ASCAP)
see Peer-Southern Organization

Blue Turtle
see Magnetic

Blues Palace (ASCAP)
539 Atlantic St.
Bethlehem, Pennsylvania 18015

BMC (ASCAP)
Address Unavailable

BMG Music (ASCAP)
1133 Sixth Avenue
New York, New York 10036

BMG Songs Inc. (ASCAP)
1133 Avenue of the Americas
New York, New York 10036

Bob-a-Lew Songs (ASCAP)
P.O. Box 8031
Universal City, California 91608

Bogam (ASCAP)
Address Unavailable

Bolland and Bolland (Netherlands)
Address Unavailable

Bona Relations Music (BMI)
see WB Music Corp.

List of Publishers

Booley Boo Boo Music (ASCAP)
P.O. Box 220
524 Myrtle Avenue
Brooklyn, New York 11205

Boosey & Hawkes Inc. (ASCAP)
24 W. 57th Street
New York, New York 10019

Emily Boothe (BMI)
2910 Poston Ave.
Nashville, Tennessee 37203

Bouillabaisse Music (BMI)
see MCA, Inc.

Bourne Co. (ASCAP)
437 Fifth Avenue
New York, New York 10016

Bovina Music, Inc. (ASCAP)
c/o Mae Attaway
330 W. 56th Street, Apt. 12F
New York, New York 10019

Brassheart Music (BMI)
c/o Jeri K. Hull, Jr.
5970 Airdrome Street
Los Angeles, California 90035

Bring the Noize Music (BMI)
see Def American Songs

Brio Blues (ASCAP)
see Almo Music Corp.

Broadhead (BMI)
see WB Music Corp.

Broken Plate Music Inc. (ASCAP)
c/o Stuart Silfen, Esq.
488 Madison Avenue
New York, New York 10022

Brooklyn Dust (ASCAP)
see Def Jam

Brother Jumbo Music (ASCAP)
c/o Gelfand Rennert & Feldman
1880 Century Park E.
Suite 900
Los Angeles, California 90067

Brother Music (BMI)
see BMG Music

Bobby Brown (ASCAP)
see EMI-April Music Inc.

Brown Foot Publishing (BMI)
P.O. Box 31
Chatham, New York 12037

Buffalo Music Factory (BMI)
Address Unavailable

Bug Music (BMI)
Bug Music Group
6777 Hollywood Blvd., 9th Fl.
Hollywood, California 90028

Bumstead (SOCAN)
1616 W. 3rd Avenue
Vancouver, British Columbia V6J1K2
Canada

Burbank Plaza (ASCAP)
c/o Filmtrax Copyright Holdings
3808 Riverside Dr.
Burbank, California 91505

Burlington Music Corp. (ASCAP)
539 W. 25th Street
New York, New York 10001

Gary Burr Music (ASCAP)
see MCA Music

Buttnugget Publishing (ASCAP)
207 1/2 First Avenue S.
Seattle, Washington 98104

C

Meryn Cadell (SOCAN)
see Intrepid Music Group (SOCAN)

Cadillac Pink Music (BMI)
see Atlantic Music Corp.

Calogie Music (ASCAP)
see Warner-Chappell Music

Tevin Campbell Music (ASCAP)
see Gratitude Sky Music, Inc.

Careers-BMG
see BMG Music

M. Carey Songs
see Sony Songs

Casa David (ASCAP)
see Jac Music Co., Inc.

Cayman Music Inc. (ASCAP)
  Music Administrative Corp.
  c/o Herzog & Straus
  155 E. 55th Street
  New York, New York 10222

Ceros (BMI)
  see Bug Music

C'est Music (ASCAP)
  see Quackenbush Music, Ltd.

Champion Music Corp. (BMI)
  c/o MCA Music
  445 Park Avenue
  New York, New York 10022

Chappell & Co., Inc. (ASCAP)
  810 Seventh Avenue
  New York, New York 10019

Chariscourt Ltd. (ASCAP)
  see Almo Music Corp.

Charm Trap Music (BMI)
  see EMI-Blackwood Music Inc.

Cherry Lane Music Co., Inc. (ASCAP)
  110 Midland Avenue
  Port Chester, New York 10573

Chi-Boy (ASCAP)
  c/o Schwartz & Farquharson
  9107 Wilshire Blvd., Suite 300
  Beverly Hills, California 90216

Chips Moman (BMI)
  P.O. Box 3145
  Memphis, Tennessee 38103

Christian Burial Music (ASCAP)
  c/o The New York End Ltd.
  143 W. 69th Street, Suite 2A
  New York, New York 10023

Chrysalis Music Corp. (ASCAP)
  Chrysalis Music Group
  645 Madison Avenue
  New York, New York 10022

Class Clown Music (ASCAP)
  315 W. 57th Street
  New York, New York 10019

Leonard Cohen Stranger Music Inc. (BMI)
  c/o Keller Lynch
  146 W. 75th Street
  New York, New York 10023

Cole-Clivilles (ASCAP)
  see Virgin Music, Inc.

Coleision (BMI)
  see EMI-Blackwood Music Inc.

Colgems-EMI Music Inc. (ASCAP)
  see Screen Gems-EMI Music Inc.

Collins Court Music, Inc. (ASCAP)
  P.O. Box 121407
  Nashville, Tennessee 37212

Color Me Blind Music (ASCAP)
  see Almo Music Corp.

Colored Folks Music (ASCAP)
  203 Martin's Lane
  Rockville, Maryland 20850

Colter Bay Music (BMI)
  see Irving Music Inc.

Controversy Music (ASCAP)
  c/o Manatt, Phelps, Rothenberg
  Att: Lee Phillips
  11355 W. Olympic Blvd.
  Los Angeles, California 90064

Copick Music (ASCAP)
  see Peer-Southern Organization

Copyright Management Inc. (BMI)
  1102 17th Ave So.
  Nashville, Tennessee 37082

Corner Club Music-Canada (SOCAN)
  Address Unavailable

Cota Music (BMI)
  see Warner-Chappell Music

Cotillion Music Inc. (BMI)
  75 Rockefeller Plaza, 2nd Fl.
  New York, New York 10019

Count Chocula Music (BMI)
  see Warner-Chappell Music

Creeping Death Music (ASCAP)
  see Cherry Lane Music Co., Inc.

List of Publishers

CRGI (BMI)
c/o CBS (Sony Records)
666 5th Ave.
New York City, New York 10103

Cri Cri Music (BMI)
see Island Music

Criterion Music Corp. (ASCAP)
6124 Selma Avenue
Hollywood, California 90028

D

D & M Publishing (BMI)
3575 Colfax Street
Gary, Indiana 46408

D.A.R.P. Music (ASCAP)
see Diva One

Dave & Darlene Music (ASCAP)
c/o Evan Dando
79 Minot Street
Dorchester, Massachusetts 02122

Daywin Music, Inc. (BMI)
c/o Six Continents Music
Publishing, Inc.
8304 Beverly Blvd.
Los Angeles, California 90048

Deb Mix Music (ASCAP)
see EMI Music Publishing, Ltd.

Deerfield Court Music (BMI)
see Tree Publishing Co., Inc.

Def American Songs (BMI)
298 Elizabeth Street
New York, New York 10012

Def Jam (ASCAP)
5 University Place
New York, New York 10003

Deshufflin' Inc.
c/o Michael Tannen, Esq.
36 E. 61st Street
New York, New York 10021

Deswing Mob (ASCAP)
see EMI-April Music Inc.

Devon Square Music (ASCAP)
see MPL Communications Inc.

Diamond Struck Music (BMI)
see MCA Music

Discharge Music (BMI)
see MCA Music

Walt Disney Music Co. (ASCAP)
350 S. Buena Vista Street
Burbank, California 91521

Diva One (ASCAP)
Gelfand, Rennert & Feldman
c/o Michael Bivens
1880 Century Park East, Ste. 900
Los Angeles, California 90067

Diva 1 Music (ASCAP)
see Spectrum VII

Dixie Stars Music (ASCAP)
see MCA Music

Dodgy Music (ASCAP)
see EMI Music Publishing, Ltd.

Dog Turner Music (ASCAP)
see EMI Music Publishing, Ltd.

Dollarz N Sense Musick (BMI)
see Sony Tunes

Donril Music (ASCAP)
see Zomba House

Dorff Songs (ASCAP)
Address unavailable

Dreamhouse (England)
Address Unavailable

Dresden China Music (ASCAP)
see Warner-Chappell Music

Drumlin Ltd. (England)
Address Unavailable

Dry Fly Music (BMI)
see Bug Music

Ronnie Dunn Music (BMI)
see Tree Publishing Co., Inc.

Dyad Music, Ltd. (BMI)
c/o Mason & Co.
75 Rockefeller Plaza
New York, New York 10019

E

E/A (BMI)
c/o Warner-Tamerlane
9000 Sunset Blvd.
Los Angeles, California 90069

Edge o' the Woods (ASCAP)
1214 16th Ave. South
Nashville, Tennessee 37212

Edisto Sound (BMI)
see CRGI

Ed's Quality Music (BMI)
9 Parsons Street
San Francisco, California 94118

Edward Grant (ASCAP)
2910 Poston Ave.
Nashville, Tennessee 37203

E.G. Music, Inc. (BMI)
161 W. 54th Street
New York, New York 10019

Emerald River Music (BMI)
see MCA Music

EMI-April Music Inc. (ASCAP)
49 E. 52nd Street
New York, New York 10022

EMI-Blackwood Music Inc. (BMI)
1350 Avenue of the Americas
23rd Fl.
New York, New York 10019

EMI Golden Torch Music (ASCAP)
see EMI Music Publishing, Ltd.

EMI Songs Ltd.
Address Unavailable

EMI Waterford Music (ASCAP)
see EMI Music Publishing, Ltd.

End of Music (BMI)
see Virgin Music, Inc.

Endless Frogs Music (ASCAP)
see Bug Music

Englishtown (BMI)
see Warner-Chappell Music

Enough to Contend With (BMI)
see Def American Songs

Ensign Music Corp. (BMI)
c/o Sidney Herman
1 Gulf & Western Plaza
New York, New York 10023

Entertainment Management Services Inc.
(BMI)
c/o Jef Scott
1223 Wilshire Blvd.
Suite 543
Santa Monica, California 90403

Eric B. & Rakim Music (ASCAP)
see EMI Music Publishing, Ltd.

ERN Kneesea Music (ASCAP)
see EMI Music Publishing, Ltd.

Estefan Music (ASCAP)
see Foreign Imported

Eye Cue Music (ASCAP)
see Almo Music Corp.

F

Faithful Werks Music (BMI)
see EMI Music Publishing, Ltd.

Falling Sky Music (ASCAP)
see BMG Songs Inc.

Falterious
see Polygram Music Publishing Inc.

Famous Monsters Music (BMI)
140 E. Seventh Street
New York, New York 10009

Famous Music Corp. (ASCAP)
Gulf & Western Industries, Inc.
1 Gulf & Western Plaza
New York, New York 10023

Feat Music (ASCAP)
c/o Loeb & Loeb
10100 Santa Monica Blvd.
Suite 2200
Los Angeles, California 90067

B. Feldman & Co., Ltd. (ASCAP)
c/o Abels, Clark & Osterberg
224 E. 50th Street
New York, New York 10022

List of Publishers

Fiction Songs U.S. Inc. (ASCAP)
850 7th Avenue
Suite 505
New York, New York 10019

First Release Music Publishing (BMI)
6124 Selma Avenue
Hollywood, California 90028

Flawfactor (BMI)
see Longitude Music

Danny Flowers (BMI)
Address Unavailable

Flyte Tyme Tunes (ASCAP)
c/o Avant Garde Music Publishing
9229 Sunset Blvd., Suite 311
Los Angeles, California 90069

Foreign Imported (BMI)
8921 S.W. Tenth Terrace
Miami, Florida 33174

Forerunner (ASCAP)
P.O. Box 120657
Nashville, Tennessee 37212

Foreshadow Songs, Inc. (BMI)
P.O. Box 120657
Nashville, Tennessee 37212

Fox Film Music Corp. (BMI)
c/o Twentieth Century Fox Film Corp
P.O. Box 900
Beverly Hills, California 90213

Full Keel (ASCAP)
4450 Lakeside Dr., Ste. 200
Burbank, California 91505

Funky Metal (ASCAP)
see Almo Music Corp.

G

Gamble-Huff Music (ASCAP)
see Mighty Three Music

Gasoline Alley Music (BMI)
see MCA Music

Geffen Music (ASCAP)
see MCA, Inc.

Get Out Songs (BMI)
see EMI Music Publishing, Ltd.

Getarealjob Music (ASCAP)
c/o Studio One Artists
P.O. Box 5824
Bethesda, Maryland 20814

Gibb Brothers Music (BMI)
see Unichappell Music Inc.

GID Music Inc. (ASCAP)
P.O. Box 120249
Nashville, Tennessee 37212

Gimme Half Publishing (ASCAP)
Attn: David Cook
931 N. Tularosa Drive
Los Angeles, California 90026

Girlfriend Music (ASCAP)
c/o Manual Parish
2152 73rd Street
Brooklyn, New York 11204

Gladys Music (ASCAP)
see Chappell & Co., Inc.

Glitterbest Music (BMI)
see BMG Songs Inc.

Godhap Music (BMI)
see Virgin Music, Inc.

Golden Reed Music (ASCAP)
Box 121081
1013 16th Avenue S.
Nashville, Tennessee 37202

Golden Rule Music (BMI)
c/o J.C. Cobb
5353 Indiana Avenue
Chicago, Illinois 60615

Michael H. Goldsen, Inc. (ASCAP)
6124 Selma Avenue
Hollywood, California 90028

Grabbitt (BMI)
54 Wall Street
Staten Island, New York 10301

Gradington Music (ASCAP)
see Warner-Chappell Music

Granary Music (BMI)
c/o Linda Clark
P.O. Box 1304
Burbank, California 91507

Gratitude Sky Music, Inc. (ASCAP)
c/o Gelfand
2062 Union Street
San Francisco, California 94123

Great Cumberland Music (BMI)
see MCA Music

Great Eastern Music (BMI)
c/o Jess S. Morgan & Co. Inc.
5750 Wilshire Blvd.
Los Angeles, California 90036

Great Z's Music (ASCAP)
see Hollywood Boulevard Music

Green Skirt Music (BMI)
see Kear Music

Guns N' Roses Music (ASCAP)
see Cherry Lane Music Co., Inc.

Gunsmoke Music Publishers (ASCAP)
see Pow Wow Records, Inc.

H

Hampstead Heath Music Publishers Ltd.
(ASCAP)
7505 Jerez Court, Suite E
Rancho La Costa
Carlsbad, California 92008

Hamstein Music (BMI)
c/o Bill Ham
P.O. Box 19647
Houston, Texas 77024

Hanseatic Music (ASCAP)
see Intersong, USA Inc.

Happy Valley Music (BMI)
1 Camp Street
Cambridge, Massachusetts 02140

Hardscratch Music (BMI)
see Irving Music Inc.

Harrick Music Inc. (BMI)
7764 N.W. 71st Street
Miami, Florida 33166

Harrindur Music (BMI)
see Ensign Music Corp.

Harvey (England)
Address Unavailable

Steve Harvey Music (ASCAP)
see EMI Music Publishing, Ltd.

Hayes Street (ASCAP)
see Almo Music Corp.

Headlift Music (BMI)
see Warner-Chappell Music

Heart Street (ASCAP)
14300 TerraBelle St. #44
Panorama City, California 91402

Heritage Hill Music (ASCAP)
see Warner-Chappell Music

Hidden Pun (BMI)
1841 Broadway
New York, New York 10023

Himmasongs (ASCAP)
Address Unavailable

Hit & Run Music (ASCAP)
1841 Broadway, Suite 411
New York, New York 10023

Hit List (ASCAP)
The Music Group
40 W. 57th St. Ste. 1515
New York, New York 10019

Hollywood Boulevard Music (ASCAP)
11800 Laughton Way
Northridge, California 91326

Hollywood Pictures Music (ASCAP)
see Walt Disney Music Co.

Holmes Creek Music (BMI)
see Irving Music Inc.

Holpic Music (BMI)
see Walt Disney Music Co.

House of Fun Music (BMI)
c/o John Benitez
1775 Broadway
New York, New York 10019

Howie Tee (BMI)
see Irving Music Inc.

List of Publishers

Howlin' Hits Music (ASCAP)
P.O. Box 19647
Houston, Texas 77224

Patti Hurt Music (ASCAP)
see Warner-Chappell Music

I

Imago Songs (ASCAP)
152 W. 57th Street
New York, New York 10019

In the Air Music (BMI)
see MCA Music

In This World Music (BMI)
see Warner-Chappell Music

Incomplete Music (BMI)
1841 Broadway
New York, New York 10023

Index Music (ASCAP)
c/o Radall, Nadell, Fine & Weinber
1775 Broadway
New York, New York 10019

Innocent Bystander Music (ASCAP)
207 1/2 First Avenue S.
Seattle, Washington 98104

Inspector Barlow (ASCAP)
see Bug Music

Intersong, USA Inc.
c/o Chappell & Co., Inc.
810 Seventh Avenue
New York, New York 10019

Intrepid Music Group (SOCAN)
65 Jefferson Avenue
Suite 205
Toronto, Ontario M6K1B
Canada

I.R.S. (BMI)
Address Unavailable

Irving Music Inc. (BMI)
1358 N. La Brea
Hollywood, California 90028

Isabug Music (ASCAP)
see Warner-Chappell Music

Island Music (BMI)
c/o Mr. Lionel Conway
6525 Sunset Blvd.
Hollywood, California 90028

It's Ceeceetee Music (BMI)
see EMI Music Publishing, Ltd.

J

J-88 Music (ASCAP)
see MCA Music

Jac Music Co., Inc. (ASCAP)
5253 Lankershim Blvd.
North Hollywood, California 91601

Jalma (ASCAP)
c/o Thomas Waits
9348 Civic Drive, Suite 101
Beverly Hills, California 90210

Rick James Music (BMI)
3500 West Olive
Burbank, California 91505

Jazz Merchant Music (ASCAP)
see Zomba Enterprises, Inc.

JMV Music Inc. (ASCAP)
Attn: James M. Vest
115 Timber Hills
Hendersonville, Tennessee 37075

Jo Skin (ASCAP)
see Zomba Enterprises, Inc.

Jobete Music Co., Inc. (ASCAP)
Att: Erlinda N. Barrios
6255 Sunset Blvd., Suite 1600
Hollywood, California 90028

Joe Public Music (BMI)
see Ensign Music Corp.

Lucy Jones Music (BMI)
see Bug Music

Josh-Nick Music (ASCAP)
Attn: Frank Myers
112 Tamasi Shores
Gallatin, Tennessee 37066

Juene Music-France
Address Unavailable

Just Cuts Music (ASCAP)
  see Warner-Chappell Music

Juters Publishing Co. (BMI)
  c/o Funzalo Music
  Att: Mike's Management
  445 Park Avenue, 7th Fl.
  New York, New York 10022

K

Kazoom (ASCAP)
  see MCA Music

Kear Music (BMI)
  Division of La Face, Inc.
  c/o Carter Turner & Co.
  9229 Sunset Blvd.
  Los Angeles, California 90069

R. Kelly Music (BMI)
  see Zomba Enterprises, Inc.

Kharatroy Music (ASCAP)
  see Chrysalis Music Corp.

Kinetic Diamond (ASCAP)
  513 Hill Road
  Nashville, Tennessee 37220

Kings Kid (BMI)
  see WB Music Corp.

Kipteez Music (ASCAP)
  see EMI Music Publishing, Ltd.

Kumumba Music Publishers (ASCAP)
  see Warner-Chappell Music

Kung Fu Grip Music (BMI)
  see BMG Songs Inc.

L

La Lennoxa Music (ASCAP)
  see BMG Songs Inc.

Last Song Music (ASCAP)
  9520 W. 47th Street
  Brookfield, Illinois 60518

Latino Buggerveil Music (ASCAP)
  see Warner-Chappell Music

Sidney Lawrence Company
  Address Unavailable

Layng Martine Jr. Songs (BMI)
  305 Sutherland Avenue
  Nashville, Tennessee 37205

Leeds Music Corp. (ASCAP)
  c/o Mr. John McKellen
  445 Park Avenue
  New York, New York 10022

Leftover Soupped Music (ASCAP)
  see Warner-Chappell Music

Oliver Leiber Music (ASCAP)
  see Virgin Music, Inc.

Lentle Music (BMI)
  see EMI Music Publishing, Ltd.

Leo Sun (ASCAP)
  see EMI-April Music Inc.

Lew-Bob Music (BMI)
  see Bob-a-Lew Songs

LFR Music (ASCAP)
  2541 Nicollet Avenue, S.
  Minneapolis, Minnesota 55404

Lilbert Music (Jamaica)
  Address Unavailable

Linda's Boys Music (BMI)
  see WB Music Corp.

Lion Hearted Music
  see EMI-April Music Inc.

Liryco's Music (BMI)
  see Irving Music Inc.

Little Maestro Music (BMI)
  see Warner-Chappell Music

L.L. Cool J Music (ASCAP)
  see Def Jam

Llee Corp. (BMI)
  c/o Lee V. Eastman
  39 W. 54th Street
  New York, New York 10019

Loggy Bayou Music (ASCAP)
  1303 Saturn Drive
  Nashville, Tennessee 37217

155

List of Publishers

Long Acre Music (SESAC)
see Warner-Chappell Music

Longitude Music (BMI)
c/o Windswept Pacific Entertainment
Co.
4450 Lakeside Drive, Suite 200
Burbank, California 91505

Love Tribe Music (ASCAP)
see MCA Music

Lyle Lovett (ASCAP)
c/o Michael H. Goldsen Inc.
6124 Selma Avenue
Hollywood, California 90028

Luella Music (ASCAP)
see Almo Music Corp.

M

Maanami (ASCAP)
see EMI-April Music Inc.

Madfly Music (ASCAP)
see Warner-Chappell Music

Major Bob Music (ASCAP)
1109 17th Avenue South
Nashville, Tennessee 37212

Mardago Music (BMI)
see Peer-Southern Organization

Eric Martin Music (ASCAP)
see EMI Music Publishing, Ltd.

Matak Music (ASCAP)
see MCA Music

Mattie Ruth (ASCAP)
1010 16th Ave. South
Nashville, Tennessee 37212

May 12th Music Inc. (BMI)
Division of Whitfield Records Inc.
901 Westbourne Drive
Los Angeles, California 90069

Maypop Music (BMI)
Att: Maggie Cavender
803 18th Avenue, S.
Nashville, Tennessee 37203

MCA, Inc. (ASCAP)
c/o Mr. John McKellen
445 Park Avenue
New York, New York 10022

MCA Music (ASCAP)
Division of MCA Inc.
445 Park Avenue
New York, New York 10022

MDL Publishing (BMI)
see Hit List

Me Good (ASCAP)
15 Remsen Ave.
Roslyn, New York 11576

Medicine Hat Music (ASCAP)
c/o Gelfand, Rennert & Feldman
Att: Babbie Green
1880 Century Park, E., No. 900
Los Angeles, California 90067

Metal Machine Music
Address Unavailable

Midsummer Music (ASCAP)
see EMI-April Music Inc.

Mighty Three Music (BMI)
c/o Earl Shelton
309 S. Broad Street
Philadelphia, Pennsylvania 19107

Mijac Music (BMI)
c/o Warner Tamerlane
Publishing Corp.
900 Sunset Blvd., Penthouse
Los Angeles, California 90069

Mike Ten (BMI)
see Diva One

Milene Music Co. (ASCAP)
see Acuff-Rose Publications Inc.

Militeer Music (ASCAP)
see Warner-Chappell Music

Milk Money Music (ASCAP)
c/o Segel & Goldman Inc.
9126 Sunset Blvd.
Los Angeles, California 90069

Millhouse (BMI)
see Welk Music Group

Mills Music Inc. (ASCAP)
  see Belwin-Mills Publishing Corp.

Mr. Bolton's Music (BMI)
  c/o David Feinstein
  120 E. 34th Street, Suite 7F
  New York, New York 10011

Mister Charlie Music (BMI)
  see Warner-Chappell Music

Mix-A-Lot Music (ASCAP)
  see Polygram Music Publishing Inc.

Mizmo Music (BMI)
  see EMI Music Publishing, Ltd.

MLE Music (ASCAP)
  see Almo Music Corp.

Modern Science Music (ASCAP)
  P.O. Box 480213
  Los Angeles, California 90048

Moebetoblame Music (BMI)
  1990 Bundy Drive
  Los Angeles, California 90025

Moline Valley (ASCAP)
  2132 No. Tremont
  Chicago, Illinois 60614

Moo Maison (ASCAP)
  see MCA, Inc.

Moo Music (ASCAP)
  see Dave & Darlene Music

Moon & Stars Music (BMI)
  see Cotillion Music Inc.

More Gliss Music (BMI)
  see Irving Music Inc.

Morgan Creek Music (ASCAP)
  see I.R.S.

Edwin H. Morris
  Address Unavailable

Gary Morris Music (ASCAP)
  Att: Gary Morris
  Rt. 3
  Hunting Creek Road
  Franklin, Tennessee 37064

Steveland Morris Music (ASCAP)
  4616 Magnolia Boulevard
  Burbank, California 91505

Morrissette Music (ASCAP)
  see EMI Music Publishing, Ltd.

Moseka Music (ASCAP)
  940 St. Nicholas Avenue
  Apt. 5E
  New York, New York 10032

Mountain Green Music (BMI)
  see Warner-Chappell Music

Mow B' Jow Music (BMI)
  see Sony Tunes

MPL Communications Inc. (ASCAP)
  c/o Lee Eastman
  39 W. 54th Street
  New York, New York 10019

MSC International (BMI)
  P.O. Box 681
  Stephensville, Texas 76401

Muckleroy Music (ASCAP)
  P.O. Box 121994
  Nashville, Tennessee 37212

Murrah (BMI)
  1025 16th Ave. South, Ste. 102
  P.O. Box 121623
  Nashville, Tennessee 37212

Music by Candlelight
  Address Unavailable

Music Corp. of America (BMI)
  see MCA, Inc.

Mustaine Music (BMI)
  see Screen Gems-EMI Music Inc.

Muy Bueno Music (BMI)
  1000 18th Street, S.
  Nashville, Tennessee 37212

Myrt & Chuck's Boy Music (ASCAP)
  2004 Cromwell Drive
  Nashville, Tennessee 37215

N

N-The Water Publishing (ASCAP)
  12337 Jones Road
  Suite 100
  Houston, Texas 77070

List of Publishers

NAH Music (ASCAP)
c/o Levine & Epstein
485 Madison Avenue
New York, New York 10022

Nasty Man Music (ASCAP)
see Shocklee

Naughty (ASCAP)
see Jobete Music Co., Inc.

Nelana Music (BMI)
c/o Fishbach & Fishbach
1925 Century Park, E., Suite 1260
Los Angeles, California 90067

New Hidden Valley Music Co. (ASCAP)
c/o Ernst & Whinney
1875 Century Park, E., No. 2200
Los Angeles, California 90067

New Perspective Publishing, Inc. (ASCAP)
see Avant Garde Music

New School Music (ASCAP)
see Zomba Enterprises, Inc.

Randy Newman Music (ASCAP)
c/o Gelfand, Rennert & Feldman
1880 Century Park, E., Suite 900
Los Angeles, California 90067

Night Garden Music (BMI)
c/o Unichappell Music, Inc.
810 Seventh Avenue, 32nd Fl.
New York, New York 10019

The Night Rainbow Music (ASCAP)
see Almo Music Corp.

No Fences Music (BMI)
see EMI Music Publishing, Ltd.

Nocturnal Eclipse Music (BMI)
see Dyad Music, Ltd.

Noiseneta Music (BMI)
see Ensign Music Corp.

Kenny Nolan Publishing Co. (ASCAP)
c/o Peter C. Bennett
9060 Santa Monica Blvd., Suite 300
Los Angeles, California 90069

Now Sounds Music (BMI)
1880 Century Park, E., 9th Fl.
Los Angeles, California 90067

NRG Music (ASCAP)
see Warner-Chappell Music

NTV Music (England)
Address Unavailable

Nubian Beat Music, Inc. (ASCAP)
P.O. Box 20413
Columbus Circle
New York, New York 10023

O

O-Tex (BMI)
see Muy Bueno Music

Oakfield Avenue Music Ltd. (BMI)
c/o David Gotterer
Mason & Co.
75 Rockefeller Plaza, Suite 1800
New York, New York 10019

Of the Fire Music (ASCAP)
c/o Daniel Zanes
117 Pembroke Street
Boston, Massachusetts 02118

Ohoo Music (BMI)
Address Unavailable

One Four Three
see Warner-Chappell Music

Oooeee Music (ASCAP)
see BMG Songs Inc.

O'Ryan Music, Inc (ASCAP)
2910 Poston Ave
Nashville, Tennessee 37203

Overboard Music
3432 La Sombra Drive
Los Angeles, California 90068

P

Padre Hotel Music (BMI)
see BMG Songs Inc.

Martin Page (ASCAP)
c/o WB Music
9000 Sunset Blvd.
Los Angeles, California 90069

Panther Music Corp. (ASCAP)
c/o Hudson Bay Music Co.
1619 Broadway, 11th Fl.
New York, New York 10019

Partner (BMI)
see Polygram Music Publishing Inc.

Pebbitone Music (ASCAP)
see Diva One

Pecot Music (ASCAP)
see EMI Music Publishing, Ltd.

Peer International Corp. (BMI)
see Peer-Southern Organization

Peer-Southern Organization
1740 Broadway
New York, New York 10019

Peermusic Ltd. (BMI)
see Peer-Southern Organization

Pentagon Lipservice Music (BMI)
see Hit & Run Music

Phantom (ASCAP)
see Warner-Chappell Music

Pillarview
Address Unavailable

Pink Pig Music (BMI)
c/o Funky But Music
P.O. Box 1770
Hendersonville, Tennessee 37075

Pink Smoke Music (BMI)
see EMI Music Publishing, Ltd.

Pitchford (BMI)
1880 Century Park
Los Angeles, California 90067

PJA Music (ASCAP)
see EMI Music Publishing, Ltd.

Playful Music (BMI)
see Warner-Chappell Music

Playhard Music (ASCAP)
2434 Main Street
Santa Monica, California 90405

Poet Tree Music (ASCAP)
see Blackhawk Music Co.

Polygram International (ASCAP)
see Polygram Music Publishing Inc.

Polygram Music Publishing Inc. (ASCAP)
Att: Brian Kelleher
c/o Polygram Records Inc.
810 Seventh Avenue
New York, New York 10019

Ponder Heart Music (BMI)
see Irving Music Inc.

Pop's Morgan Music (BMI)
see I.R.S.

Post Oak (BMI)
see Tree Publishing Co., Inc.

Pow Wow Records, Inc. (ASCAP)
1776 Broadway
New York, New York 10019

Power Metal Music (BMI)
2210 Raper Blvd.
Arlington, Texas 76013

PPC Songs (ASCAP)
2121 Avenue of the Stars
Suite 3200
Los Angeles, California 90067

Elvis Presley Music, Inc. (BMI)
c/o Chappell & Co.
810 Seventh Avenue
New York, New York 10019

Prize Pagoda Music (ASCAP)
532 La Guardia Place, #383
New York, New York 10012

Promopub BV
Address Unavailable

Prophet Sharing Music (ASCAP)
4049 Edenhurst Avenue
Los Angeles, California 90039

PSO Ltd. (ASCAP)
see Peer-Southern Organization

Putz Tunes (BMI)
c/o The Abacus Co.
4076 McLaughlin Avenue
Los Angeles, California 90066

List of Publishers

Q

Quackenbush Music, Ltd. (ASCAP)
  c/o Gelfand, Rennert & Feldman
  Att: Babbie Green
  1880 Century Park, E., No. 900
  Los Angeles, California 90067

Queen Music Ltd. (BMI)
  see Beechwood Music Corp.

R

R & H Music Co. (BMI)
  1633 Broadway
  New York, New York 10019

Rain Light Music (ASCAP)
  see Bug Music

Rainyville Music (BMI)
  see Island Music

Ramal Music Co. (BMI)
  5999 Bear Creek Rd. No. 304
  Bedford Heights, Ohio 44146

Ranch Rock (ASCAP)
  see WB Music Corp.

Rated RT Music (ASCAP)
  see Flyte Tyme Tunes

Real World Music (ASCAP)
  see Hidden Pun

Really Useful Group (ASCAP)
  see Screen Gems-EMI Music Inc.

Realsongs (ASCAP)
  Address Unavailable

Reata Publishing Inc. (ASCAP)
  9000 Sunset Blvd.
  Los Angeles, California 90069

Rebel Waltz Music (ASCAP)
  see Sony Tunes

Resaca Beach Music (BMI)
  see Warner-Chappell Music

Reunion (ASCAP)
  see EMI-April Music Inc.

RHO Music (ASCAP)
  see Zomba Enterprises, Inc.

Rhyme Syndicate (ASCAP)
  2825 Dunbar Drive
  Riverside, California 92503

Rightsong Music Inc. (BMI)
  see Chappell & Co., Inc.

Risque Situe Music (BMI)
  see Warner-Chappell Music

Riverstone (ASCAP)
  120 30th Avenue N.
  Nashville, Tennessee 37203

RMG Music (ASCAP)
  see EMI Music Publishing, Ltd.

Robinette Music (ASCAP)
  see Polygram Music Publishing Inc.

Rock Music (BMI)
  c/o Beechwood Music Corp.
  6255 Sunset Blvd.
  Hollywood, California 90028

Rok Godz (ASCAP)
  P.O. Box 1910
  Los Angeles, California 90028

Rom Music (ASCAP)
  see EMI Music Publishing, Ltd.

Ronnie Runs Music (ASCAP)
  see EMI Music Publishing, Ltd.

Ruthless Attack Muzick (ASCAP)
  3126 Locust Ridge Circle
  Valencia, California 91354

S

Saba Seven Music (BMI)
  see Ensign Music Corp.

Sailor Music (ASCAP)
  c/o Gregory Fischbach
  2029 Century Park, E.
  North Tower, Suite 1370
  Los Angeles, California 90067

Samosonian Music (ASCAP)
  see Warner-Chappell Music

Savage Conquest Music (ASCAP)
  332 Madison Drive, #3R
  Hoboken, New Jersey 07030

Don Schlitz Music (ASCAP)
P.O. Box 120594
Nashville, Tennessee 37212

Screen Gems-EMI Music Inc. (BMI)
6255 Sunset Blvd., 12th Fl.
Hollywood, California 90028

Sea Foam Music Co. (BMI)
200 W. 58th Street, #5E
New York, New York 10019

Second Generation Rooney Tunes (BMI)
see MCA Music

Sesame Street Inc. (ASCAP)
c/o Children's Television Workshop
1 Lincoln Plaza
New York, New York 10023

Seventh Son Music Inc. (ASCAP)
c/o Glen Campbell Enterprises Ltd.
10351 Santa Monica Blvd,, Suite 300
Los Angeles, California 90025

Shadows International (BMI)
see Zomba Enterprises, Inc.

Allen Shamblin Music (ASCAP)
see Almo Music Corp.

Shanice 4U (ASCAP)
see Gratitude Sky Music, Inc.

Alex Shartzis Music (ASCAP)
see EMI Music Publishing, Ltd.

Sheddhouse Music (ASCAP)
27 Music Circle, E.
Nashville, Tennessee 37203

Sheep in Tow Music (BMI)
see Irving Music Inc.

Shepsongs (ASCAP)
see MCA Music

Richard Shindell Music (ASCAP)
Address Unavailable

Shocklee (BMI)
John M. Gross, Esq.
51 E. 42nd St. Ste. 1601
New York, New York 10017

Short Trip Music (BMI)
see Bug Music

Siete Leguas Music (ASCAP)
see Warner-Chappell Music

Silver Angel Music Inc. (ASCAP)
c/o Franklin, Weinrib, Rudell &
Vassalo
Att: Nick Gordon
950 Third Avenue
New York, New York 10022

Silver Fiddle (ASCAP)
c/o Segel & Goldman Inc.
9200 Sunset Blvd., Suite 1000
Los Angeles, California 90069

Paul Simon Music (BMI)
1619 Broadway
New York, New York 10019

Sister Elisabeth Music (BMI)
5614 Matilisa Avenue
Van Nuys, California 91401

Six Continents Music Publishing Inc.
8304 Beverly Blvd.
Los Angeles, California 90048

Sky Garden Music (ASCAP)
see Peer-Southern Organization

Slaughter Neville Music (BMI)
see Irving Music Inc.

Sloppy Slouch Music (ASCAP)
13333 Ventura Blvd.
Suite 206
Sherman Oaks, California 91423

Slow Train Music (ASCAP)
see BMG Songs Inc.

Sluggo Songs (BMI)
c/o Jess S. Morgan & Co. Inc.
5750 Wilshire Blvd.
Los Angeles, California 90036

Smooshie Music (BMI)
see EMI Music Publishing, Ltd.

Snow Music
c/o Jess Morgan & Co., Inc.
6420 Wilshire Blvd., 19th Fl.
Los Angeles, California 90048

Tom Snow Music (BMI)
see Snow Music

List of Publishers

Snowden Music (ASCAP)
344 W. 12th Street
New York, New York 10014

So So Def Music (ASCAP)
see EMI Music Publishing, Ltd.

Curt Sobel Music (BMI)
see T-L Music

Something Stoopid Music (ASCAP)
see EMI Music Publishing, Ltd.

Sometimes You Win (ASCAP)
see Almo Music Corp.

Son Mare (BMI)
see EMI-April Music Inc.

Songs of Logic (ASCAP)
see Warner-Chappell Music

Songs of Polygram (BMI)
see Polygram Music Publishing Inc.

Sony Cross Keys Publishing Co. Inc.
c/o Donna Hilley
P.O. Box 1273
Nashville, Tennessee 37202

Sony Epic/Solar (BMI)
see Sony Songs

Sony Music Publishing (BMI)
see Sony Songs

Sony Songs (BMI)
P.O. Box 8500 (2320)
Philadelphia, Pennsylvania 19178

Sony Tree (ASCAP)
see Tree Publishing Co., Inc.

Sony Tunes (ASCAP)
c/o Tree Music International
8 Music Square West
Nashville, Tennessee 37202

Sophie's Choice Music (BMI)
1705 Warfield Drive
Nashville, Tennessee 37215

Soul Assassins Music (ASCAP)
see T-Boy

Southern Music Publishing Co., Inc.
(ASCAP)
Att: Ralph Peer, II
1740 Broadway
New York, New York 10019

Special Rider Music (ASCAP)
P.O. Box 860, Cooper Sta.
New York, New York 10276

Spectrum VII (ASCAP)
1635 Cahuenga Blvd., 6th Fl.
Hollywood, California 90028

Speeding Bullet Music (ASCAP)
c/o Jess S. Morgan & Co. Inc.
5750 Wilshire Blvd.
Los Angeles, California 90036

Spheric BV Music (ASCAP)
see Warner-Chappell Music

Spiegel Music (ASCAP)
see T-L Music

Bruce Springsteen Publishing (ASCAP)
c/o Jon Landau Management, Inc.
Att: Barbara Carr
136 E. 57th Street, No. 1202
New York, New York 10021

Spurburn Music (BMI)
see Warner-Chappell Music

Stainless Music Group
509 Madison Avenue, Suite 1810
New York, New York 10022

Starry Plough Music (BMI)
31-33 Mercer Street
Apt. 2C
New York, New York 10013

Billy Steinberg Music (ASCAP)
c/o Manatt, Phelps, Rothenberg &
Tunney
11355 W. Olympic Blvd.
Los Angeles, California 90064

Step 3 Music (ASCAP)
28128 Pacific Coast Highway, #180
Malibu, California 90265

Ray Stevens Music (BMI)
1707 Grand Avenue
Nashville, Tennessee 37212

Stigwood Music Inc. (BMI)
  see Unichappell Music Inc.

Stone Agate Music Corp. (BMI)
  6255 Sunset Blvd.
  Hollywood, California 90028

Stone Diamond Music Corp. (BMI)
  6255 Sunset Blvd., Suite 1600
  Dept. 4-7566
  Los Angeles, California 90028

Stone Jam Music (ASCAP)
  see Warner-Chappell Music

Stonebridge Music (ASCAP)
  The Bicycle Music Co.
  8075 W. Third Street, Suite 400
  Los Angeles, California 90048

Straitjacket Music (ASCAP)
  see Almo Music Corp.

Stroudavarious Music (ASCAP)
  see Warner-Chappell Music

Studio B. Music (BMI)
  see Warner-Chappell Music

Stylz Music (ASCAP)
  see MCA Music

Henry SueMay Publishing Inc. (BMI)
  c/o Lloyd Remick, Esq.
  1529 Walnut Street, 6th Fl.
  Philadelphia, Pennsylvania 19102

Al B. Sure (ASCAP)
  P.O. Box 8075
  Englewood, New Jersey 07631

Sure Fire Music Co., Inc.
  60 Music Square, W.
  Nashville, Tennessee 37203

Susan Street Music (BMI)
  see Dyad Music, Ltd.

Keith Sweat (ASCAP)
  Address Unavailable

Sweet Angel Music (ASCAP)
  c/o Michael H. Goldson, Esq.
  6124 Selma Avenue
  Hollywood, California 90028

Sword and Stone (ASCAP)
  10209 Gary Road
  Potomac, Maryland 20854

T

T-Boy
  Address Unavailable

T-L Music (ASCAP)
  c/o HBO Inc.
  1290 Avenue of the Americas
  New York, New York 10104

Tajai Music (BMI)
  see Mighty Three Music

TCF Music Publishing (ASCAP)
  Twentieth Century Fox Corp.
  c/o Mary Jo Mennella
  P.O. Box 900
  Music Dept. Bldg. 222
  Beverly Hills, California 90213

Tee Off Music (ASCAP)
  see Almo Music Corp.

Television Music Ltd. (England)
  Address Unavailable

Testatyme (ASCAP)
  see Almo Music Corp.

They Might Be Giants Music (ASCAP)
  232 N. Fifth Street
  Brooklyn, New York 11211

Third Coast Music (ASCAP)
  see Last Song Music

310 Jammin' (ASCAP)
  see Zomba Enterprises, Inc.

Through Being Cool Music (BMI)
  see Warner-Chappell Music

Thumb Sucker Music (BMI)
  see I.R.S.

Tickson Music (BMI)
  c/o Fischbach, Fischbach & Weiner
  2029 Century Park, E., Suite 1370
  Los Angeles, California 90028

Tinterette Music (BMI)
  see Ensign Music Corp.

List of Publishers

Tizbiz Music (ASCAP)
see Diva One

T.J. Music (ASCAP)
see EMI Music Publishing, Ltd.

TJT (ASCAP)
see Warner-Chappell Music

Tonopah & Tidewater Music (ASCAP)
see BMG Songs Inc.

Tough Knot Music (ASCAP)
see Warner-Chappell Music

Trailer Trash Music (ASCAP)
see BMG Songs Inc.

Tranquility Base Songs (ASCAP)
c/o Tom Shannon
5101 Whitesett Avenue
Studio City, California 91607

Treat Baker Music (SOCAN)
c/o NGB Inc.
579 Richmond St. W.
Suite 401
Toronto, Ontario M5V1Y6
Canada

Tree Publishing Co., Inc. (BMI)
P.O. Box 1273
Nashville, Tennessee 37203

Triple Star (BMI)
1875 Century Park E.
Los Angeles, California 90067

TRO-Cromwell Music Inc. (ASCAP)
10 Columbus Circle
New York, New York 10019

Dan Truman Music (BMI)
see Warner-Chappell Music

Trycep Publishing Co. (BMI)
c/o John P. Kellog, Esq.
33 Public Square, No. 810
Cleveland, Ohio 44113

Two Tuff-Enuff Publishing (BMI)
6042 Bellingham Drive
Castro Valley, California 94552

Tyrell Music Group (BMI)
8295 Sunset Blvd.
Los Angeles, California 90046

U

U/A (ASCAP)
Address Unavailable

Uncle Pete Music (BMI)
Box 161
Brentwood, Tennessee 37024

Uncle Ronnie's Music Co., Inc. (ASCAP)
1775 Broadway
New York, New York 10019

Unforgettable Songs (BMI)
Address Unavailable

Unichappell Music Inc. (BMI)
810 Seventh Avenue, 32nd Fl.
New York, New York 10019

United Lion Music Inc. (BMI)
c/o United Artists Corp.
729 Seventh Avenue
New York, New York 10019

U2 (ASCAP)
see Chappell & Co., Inc.

V

Van Halen Music (ASCAP)
Att: Gail Liss
6525 Sunset Blvd., 7th Fl.
Hollywood, California 90028

Van Warmer Music (ASCAP)
1304 Robert L. Lee Lane
Brentwood, Tennessee 37027

Vanilla Music (ASCAP)
Attn: Kathleen Anne Dorritie
85C East Broadway
Milford, Connecticut 06460

Velvet Apple Music (BMI)
Three International
8 Music Square, W.
Nashville, Tennessee 37212

Venutian Publishing Ltd (ASCAP)
see MPL Communications Inc.

VER Music (BMI)
see Warner-Chappell Music

Vermal (BMI)
see EMI-Blackwood Music Inc.

Virgin Music, Inc. (ASCAP)
Att: Ron Shoup
43 Perry Street
New York, New York 10014

Virgin Songs (BMI)
see Virgin Music, Inc.

Vomit God (ASCAP)
see Cherry Lane Music Co., Inc.

W

Waifersongs Ltd. (ASCAP)
c/o Michael C. Lesser, Esq.
225 Broadway, Suite 1915
New York, New York 10007

Wallyworld Music (ASCAP)
see Warner-Chappell Music

War Bride Music (BMI)
see EMI Music Publishing, Ltd.

Warner Brothers, Inc. (ASCAP)
9000 Sunset Blvd.
Los Angeles, California 90069

Warner-Chappell Music (ASCAP)
c/o Cathy Nolan
9000 Sunset Blvd.
Penthouse
Los Angeles, California 90069

Warner-Elektra-Asylum Music Inc. (BMI)
1815 Division Street
Nashville, Tennessee 37203

Warner-Tamerlane Publishing Corp. (BMI)
c/o Warner Brothers, Inc.
9000 Sunset Blvd.
Penthouse
Los Angeles, California 90069

Warnes Music (BMI)
see Copyright Management Inc.

Roger Waters Music (BMI)
see Pink Floyd

WB Music Corp. (ASCAP)
c/o Warner Brothers, Inc.
Att: Leslie E. Bider

9000 Sunset Blvd., Penthouse
Los Angeles, California 90069

WBM (SESAC)
see Warner Brothers, Inc.

Webo Girl (ASCAP)
see Warner-Chappell Music

Welbeck Music Corp. (ASCAP)
Total Video Music
c/o ATV Music Group
6255 Sunset Blvd., Suite 723
Hollywood, California 90028

Welk Music Group
1299 Ocean Avenue, Suite 800
Santa Monica, California 90401

Wet Sprocket Songs (ASCAP)
901 Third Street
Suite 407
Santa Monica, California 90403

Whiskey Drinkin' Music (BMI)
see Bug Music

Whistling Moon Traveler (BMI)
see Irving Music Inc.

Wild Country Music (BMI)
see Warner-Chappell Music

David N. Will (ASCAP)
see Willin' David

Willarie (ASCAP)
c/o SBK Songs
1290 Avenue of the Americas
New York, New York 10019

Willesden Music, Inc. (BMI)
c/o Zomba House
1348 Lexington Avenue
New York, New York 10028

Williamson Music Inc. (ASCAP)
see Chappell & Co., Inc.

Willin' David (BMI)
1205 16th Avenue, S.
Nashville, Tennessee 37212

Wing & Wheel (BMI)
see Irving Music Inc.

Wing It
Address Unavailable

List of Publishers

Wocka Wocka (ASCAP)
Address Unavailable

Wonderland Music Co., Inc. (BMI)
c/o Vic Guder
350 S. Buena Vista Street
Burbank, California 91521

Worldwide Anchor Music (ASCAP)
see Pow Wow Records, Inc.

Wrightchild (BMI)
see EMI-Blackwood Music Inc.

Write Treatage Music (ASCAP)
207 1/2 First Avenue S.
Seattle, Washington 98104

Writing Staff Music (ASCAP)
see Warner-Chappell Music

D. Wynn Music (ASCAP)
see Zomba Enterprises, Inc.

Y

Yellow Elephant
see Sony Tunes

You Make Me Sick I Make Music (ASCAP)
c/o Manatt Phelps Rothenberg &
Tunney
11355 W. Olympic Blvd.
Los Angeles, California 90064

Young Carny Music (ASCAP)
see Warner-Chappell Music

Z

Zavion (SOCAN)
1948 Sasamat Place
Vancouver, British Columbia V6R4A3
Canada

Zena Music (ASCAP)
P.O. Box 8470
Universal City, California 91608

Zero Productions (BMI)
c/o Clog Holdings
3300 Warner Blvd.
Burbank, California 91501

Zoe Zimmer Music (BMI)
see Fox Film Music Corp.

Zomba Enterprises, Inc. (BMI)
c/o Zomba House
1348 Lexington Avenue
New York, New York 10128

Zomba House (ASCAP)
137-139 W. 25th St, 8th Floor
New York, New York 10001

Zoo II Music (ASCAP)
4205 Hillsboro Road
Nashville, Tennessee 37215

ISBN 0-8103-8234-2

90000